Wake Up! Sober Up!

THE ROAD TO SPIRITUAL SOBRIETY

By Regina Braden, Heather Hougland, and Aisha Jenya

© 2023 Spiritbuilding Publishers.

All rights reserved. No part of this book may be reproduced in any form without the written permission of the publisher.

Published by

Spiritbuilding Publishers

9700 Ferry Road, Waynesville, OH 45068

Wake Up! Sober Up!

by Regina Braden, Heather Hougland, & Aisha Jenya

ISBN: 9781955285711

spiritbuilding.com

Introduction

Wake up, Sober Up is an eight-chapter study that challenges the reader to wake up and evaluate attitudes, behaviors and conditions which negatively impact their distinctiveness, influence, and efficacy as witnesses and disciples of Christ. Often, we are oblivious to the subtleties that chip away at our calling in Christ and the convictions we once held so dearly or those never fully realized. We become distracted by the cares of this world and find ourselves conforming to man-made ideologies and systems instead of rejecting these errors and allowing the transforming power of God's Word to keep us grounded and aligned with His will.

We may find ourselves going through the motions, unmotivated and uninspired, living day to day in ritualistic fashion without any concern for our spiritual responsibilities and obligations. However, to remain in a spiritual stupor or state of indifference and complacency will render us fruitless and useless for the work of our Lord. It's high time that we arise from the drunkenness of sin and take hold of God's gift of salvation.

This study is to encourage all along the road less traveled, the road to spiritual sobriety that ultimately leads to eternal life.

Dedication

To all who desire to awake to righteousness and remain alert, sober and vigilant as we await the coming of the Lord.

To Brother Sabin Johnson, the minister of the Watkins Rd. church of Christ where we all worship, thank you for your powerful sermons, thorough teaching, and outstanding service to God. Also, thank you for crafting this idea and challenging the three of us to work together to produce a bible study that would help others who are striving for a stronger Christian life.

> "Therefore He says: "Awake, you who sleep,
> Arise from the dead, And Christ will give you light.""
>
> Ephesians 5:14 NKJV

> "And do this, knowing the time,
> that now it is high time to awake out of sleep;
> for now our salvation is nearer
> than when we first believed."
>
> Romans 13:11 NKJV

> "Therefore let us not sleep,
> as others do, but let us watch and be sober."
>
> 1 Thessalonians 5:6 NKJV

Table of Contents

Wake Up, Sober Up!
'The Road to Spiritual Sobriety'

Chapter 1	The Walking Dead	4	*Regina Braden*
Chapter 2	The Other gods I Serve	18	*Regina Braden*
Chapter 3	Is It Worth the Cost?	29	*Aisha Jenya*
Chapter 4	The Sound of the Trumpet	43	*Aisha Jenya*
Chapter 5	Stop with the Excuses!	56	*Aisha Jenya*
Chapter 6	Accepting God's Will	71	*Heather Hougland*
Chapter 7	My Resolve	87	*Heather Hougland*
Chapter 8	Maintaining Sobriety	97	*Heather Hougland*

Chapter 1 – *The Walking Dead*

Physically alive, spiritually dead

The Walking Dead chapter title may sound like the name of a gory horror movie where brain dead zombies aimlessly wander about terrorizing others. While we will not discuss horror movies, we will seek to provide a study of the danger of being physically alive, yet day by day aimlessly wandering in a spiritually dead way disconnected from God, other Christians, and our true purpose.

Just like the zombie, we might not even know that we are aimlessly wandering because we are getting things done. We spend a lot of time, money, and effort pursuing our goals and receiving accolades, but deep down inside something is missing. True personal fulfillment is fleeting. So, although we may think we are getting the best of what this world offers to make us feel alive - if we never encounter what matters most – living a life made alive by God – then we are missing the opportunity for a relationship with the true life source.

Walking Dead

In Ephesians 2:1-6, Paul enlightens early Christians about how they were made alive in Christ.

Ephesians 2:1-6 NKJV

"And you He made alive, who were dead in trespasses and sins, in which you once walked according to the course of this world, according to the prince of the power of the air, the spirit who now works in the sons of disobedience, among whom also we all once conducted ourselves in the lusts of our flesh, fulfilling the desires of the flesh and of the mind, and were by nature children of wrath, just as the others. But God, who is rich in mercy, because of His great love with which He loved us, even when we were dead in trespasses, made us alive together with Christ (by grace you have been saved), and raised us up together, and made us sit together in the heavenly places in Christ Jesus,"

Satan is the source of dead living. Paul teaches that God's great love makes us alive with Christ and reminds us that before submitting to God, we were walking around spiritually dead. Before we were Christians, we thought we were okay. We lived in habitual sin and supported values that aligned very closely to the world, measuring success and happiness by the world's standards. The tragedy of living in a spiritually dead state is that it lulls us into a complacent mindset that is not sober or vigilant, but instead it feeds into Satan's end game of devouring Christians (1 Peter 5:8).

Like those early Christians referenced in Ephesians 2, we also can think we are just fine, but doing so with sin as an ingrained behavior that goes unacknowledged, unchecked, and unforgiven. Our lifestyles can be busy in so many ways. Sometimes we chase dreams without considering how they fit into God's will for us. On the opposite end of the spectrum, maybe we have a full checklist of tasks to finish each day, but drift numbly, just going through the motions. Both efforts can produce an empty feeling inside because we do not include room for God's will. Without God guiding our path, we miss the fulfillment of meeting our spiritual potential.

Worldly ways of trying to feel alive fail. Many industries try to help enrich our lives by selling ways to reverse the hands of time, achieve a higher purpose, or have an intense once in a lifetime heart pounding experience. It can be very tempting to tap into resources as we chase goals and try to live "our best lives" through these methods. The problem is that worldly driven solutions for "best" do not include God's standards. So, we can try the newest fad to feel alive, but the feeling does not last, it is just a short-term fix. Like much that the world offers, it only feels good for a little while. Until what is truly problematic is addressed, which could be our way of thinking, until it is changed, a lasting fix should not be expected. For example, it is not hard to imagine how bungy jumping could offer a heart pounding, exhilarating experience. We may prepare ourselves and follow the instructions in anticipation of the big jump! However, afterwards, once the adrenalin rush and happiness of surviving the jump is over, it is just over. Successfully completing a bungy jump could give the courage to do other things in life, but does not provide the depth of personal insight, help to others, or endless tools that personal examination in the light of scripture can provide to support a lifetime of courage. The success of bungy jumping might make us want to feel that thrill of accomplishment again, so we choose to try the next level of thrill seeking – maybe parachuting. As Christians, we do not have to chase accomplishment in the same way as a world under Satan's influence does and expect it to work. The world provides self-centered, self-serving solutions that look to self for the answer. This inward focus for truth is an invitation to sin in our daily lives because we alone do not hold all the answers to our problems.

Grieving the Holy Spirit starves the soul. Self-absorbed living does not please God. Ephesians 4:30 teaches that Christians are not to grieve the Holy Spirit. Habitually focusing on self, and not Christ, grieves the Holy Spirit because it promotes greater self-sufficiency and less Christ sustainability in the soul. Good fruit cannot sprout from this starvation! Galatians 5:16 and 22-23 highlight the evidence of what behaviors are present in lives consistently striving to live a life in the faith.

> *I say then: Walk in the Spirit, and you shall not fulfill the lust of the flesh. But the fruit of the Spirit is love, joy, peace, longsuffering, kindness, goodness, faithfulness, gentleness, self-control. Against such there is no law.*

When we are not producing the fruit of the Spirit, it is highly likely we are serving up damaged spiritual fruit. While we may think our spiritual flaws are hidden from others, they are not. Our character and behavior flow from what resides in our heart and will tell the truth about us.

We are Alive!

Christians are so fortunate because God planned for us even when we were not thinking about living for Him. He knew the sinful state of His people and sent Jesus to redeem us from sin. In John 15:5 it is taught that branches are powerless without Him, the vine (John 15:5).

> *I am the vine, you are the branches. He who abides in Me, and I in him, bears much fruit; for without Me you can do nothing.*

God sent Christ to give life. Thankfully, submission to the gospel call through baptism, revives the non-Christian and repentance revives the Christian from their spiritually dead states! There is a popular term that people use when talking about something they love. They say, "It gives me life". Christ actually gives us LIFE! 2 Corinthians 5:17 says,

> *Therefore, if anyone is in Christ, he is a new creation; old things have passed away; behold, all things have become new.*

Ephesians 2:1-5 teaches us that we were dead in our trespasses, it is Christ who makes us alive.

> *But God, who is rich in mercy, because of His great love*
> *with which He loved us, even when we were dead in trespasses,*
> *made us alive together with Christ (by grace you have been saved),*

Have you ever been gardening on a warm sunny day? After a while, this physical work makes you dirty, sweaty, and just plain old uncomfortable. Think about how refreshing it is to enter an air-conditioned room, shed the dirty clothes, and take that refreshing shower. The change in your state is distinctive. You change from dirty to clean and feel restored! This is how it is when we allow ourselves to be transformed into a new creation who has submitted to the will of Christ!

Dwelling and holding onto our past sins and rejections appeals to our carnal nature and does not allow us to be transformed and refreshed! It is this sinful place within that resists treating the one who rejected us or did us wrong with love. Revenge or justification feels right. Yet, God has never treated us this way. It is the very love that God feels for us, his children, that caused him to send Christ (John 3:16) to save us and give us hope for eternal life.

> *For God so loved the world that He gave His only begotten Son,*
> *that whoever believes in Him should not perish but have everlasting life.*

Romans 6:4 NKJV

> *"Therefore we were buried with Him through baptism into death,*
> *that just as Christ was raised from the dead by the glory of the Father,*
> *even so we also should walk in newness of life."*

Becoming spiritually alive starts with our obedience to the gospel by submitting to baptism, where we receive the gift of the Holy Spirit (Acts 2:38), and are finally united with Christ in a new walk.

Renewed thinking gives life! Paul teaches in Romans 8 that when Christians think worldly thoughts our minds will refuse to submit to God. We are in enmity against God, the only one that can make us alive spiritually, and we therefore cannot please Him (vs. 7-8).

> *Because the carnal mind is enmity against God;*
> *for it is not subject to the law of God, nor indeed can be.*
> *So then, those who are in the flesh cannot please God.*

When in a sinful state, our thinking is spiritually dead because it is too influenced by what the world thinks. Paul characterizes worldly thinking as being in opposition to God. Persisting in this type of thinking is rejecting God's offer to make alive that which comes through building faith in our obedience to Christ.

Romans 12:2 further teaches that the way for us to avoid conforming to the world, is to transform our thinking from worldly to Godly. We must acknowledge that our old way of thinking, prior to becoming a Christian, did not produce a righteous end because it was characterized by unspiritual reasoning. Transforming our thinking from carnal to spiritual brings the will of God to the forefront of our minds.

> *"And do not be conformed to this world, but be transformed by the renewing of your mind, that you may prove what is that good and acceptable and perfect will of God."*

This renewed way of thinking leads to better decision making and shedding our old ways. It encourages a new perspective on our purpose, life, and how to handle the situations we encounter. The old way that was separate from God did not give us peace of mind and strength of character that comes from walking in the counsel of wisdom as described in Psalms 1.

A look at the latest and hottest reality TV shows provides many examples of how one might view life from that old sinful perspective. Often the characters react to even the simplest of issues in an "over the top" dramatic way with outcomes that are not peaceful or productive – but can involve a lot of cursing and weave pulling! Yet, it would be difficult to convince them that their methods are not effective! Why? They receive what they value - fame, notoriety, and money. Yet, happiness, peace, and joy are not on that list of rewards because they are often not highly valued.

When we walk spiritually alive, we do not have to react in an emotionally fueled or cold calculated way that listens to our sinful urges on how to solve our issues. We have access to how to use the "spiritual filter" that filters our emotions based on God's word and helps us decide how to respond to life setting the priorities to which we are committed.

What is a Spiritual Filter?

A filter allows what is wanted to be separated from that which is unwanted. In a typical week, we are exposed to many different types of messages, visuals, and provocations that we process consciously and subconsciously. So, understandably some of those elements subtly slip in unnoticed and influence our thinking. The spiritual filter is where we deliberately make decisions about how we will handle these inputs. As we sort our thoughts, we ask ourselves the question of whether or not this aligns to the guidance of God's word. Consider the words of Jesus in Mark 7:20-21.

> *And He said, "What comes out of a man, that defiles a man.*
> *For from within, out of the heart of men, proceed evil thoughts…*

Whatever comes out of our mouths, in our behaviors, and in our responses shows what is lodged deep within our hearts. How is the heart controlled? Proverbs 4:23 provides an answer. It says that the heart should be guarded because everything in life is sourced from it.

> *Above all else, guard your heart,*
> *for everything you do flows from it. (NIV)*

A visual might be of an armed guard checking all those messages, visuals, and provocations at the entrance of our minds. If they have the right credentials, they can enter, if they do not then the guard blocks them from coming inside. That is literally what Christians must do! We check what we are exposed to and block what is useless, so we do not waste time dwelling on it. Our best defense is multifaceted. When we start closely monitoring what we allow in, we can reduce the junk messages to which we listen. Study, write down scriptures, memorize them, and pray about them using the courage we have gained to apply what they teach. The renewed mindset is evident when what we say, do, and think makes us distinctive from the world.

|||||||||||||||||||||||||||||||||||||||||||

Set Apart or Fitting In

Separating from sin and avoiding fitting in with the world does not refer to our physical proximity, but how closely our mindset fits in with worldly logic and reasoning. If we do not interact within society, how can we teach the gospel and show how to navigate relationships and problems in a godly way. While we live and move within our communities, we must resist being tainted by worldly desires and goals. 1 Samuel 8 records Israel's desire to be like the world and its consequences. They wanted an earthly king to rule over them. In verses 19-20 they provide their reasoning for this…

1 Samuel 8:19-20 -

> *Nevertheless the people refused to obey the voice of Samuel;*
> *and they said, "No, but we will have a king over us,*
> *that we also may be like all the nations,*
> *and that our king may judge us and go out before us and fight our battles."*

Israel wanted to be like the other nations around them and judged that having a king to go before them in battle was what they should do. In their reasoning, it seemed to be working for the neighboring nations, so it must be right and good enough for them. They preferred the rule of an earthly king over the love, protection, and provision provided by the heavenly Father!

> *And the LORD said to Samuel, "Heed the voice of the people in all that they say to you; for they have not rejected you, but <u>they have rejected Me</u>, that I should not reign over them. According to all the works which they have done since the day that I brought them up out of Egypt, even to this day—with which they have forsaken Me and served other gods—so they are doing to you also. Now therefore, heed their voice. However, you shall solemnly forewarn them, and show them the behavior of the king who will reign over them."*

Israel ignored the consequences of rejecting God just so they could have their king. In 1 Samuel 8:11-17, Samuel lists the ways the earthly king would behave. A review of this list shows that a king would take much from them. This is so different from the transparent way God wants to love and protect us.

And so, it is with many of us today. How the world sees living the "good life" can have a stronger influence on us than staying sanctified by God's higher purpose for us. 1 Peter 3:15 teaches us to *sanctify (set apart) God in our hearts*… When God is in our minds and hearts, then we will not crave what the world offers. 1 John 2:15 reminds us not to fall in love with the world or worldly things.

> *"Do not love the world or the things in the world.*
> *If anyone loves the world, the love of the Father is not in him."*

Worldly ways produce Christians who are not distinctive in living, talking, and priority setting. When we desire the recognition and acceptance of the world over the love and protection God provides, then we are loving the world more than God. Although we may not think about it this way, we are telling God that we prefer other stuff above Him. So, when we choose organizational meetings and little league games over the set times of worship and bible study, then we are obeying worldly commitments rather than serving God. It may seem easier to occasionally plan to miss worship instead of taking a stand for Christ by disappointing associates, colleagues, friends, family, and sometimes even our kids, by making decisions to miss practices. The truth is that while it may seem easier in that moment to comply, the long-term consequences of these decisions can be far graver because we miss gospel messages and fellowships designed to build our faith. Further, these actions also teach others that we consider designated times of worship or formal bible study as optional and not critical to our spiritual health.

|||||||||||||||||||||||||||||||||||||||||||

Winning the internal battle between the flesh and Spirit.

Paul constantly reminded first century Christians that walking according to the Spirit means deciding not to serve our flesh.

Galatians 5:16
I say then: Walk in the Spirit, and you shall not fulfill the lust of the flesh.

There is a decision to be made on who will be served. Romans 6:19 highlights that the struggle is real!

*"For the good that I will to do, I do not do;
but the evil I will not to do, that I practice."*

Satan wages a war where the prize is control of Christians souls. We can think we want to do good, but evil is always there as an option. As sober Christians we cannot take this for granted by assuming that we always make the right choices. Like soldiers with military strategies, we must use our strategies and resources to manage the spiritual battles that we fight. This is not something that will just naturally happen. It takes our conscious effort and thoughtful choice to win the internal battles and wars. The Holy Spirit works the understanding of the truths of Scripture within us to overcome those ungodly desires. In this battle we may feel like the funny depictions we may have seen where an angel sits on one shoulder and a devil sits on the other shoulder. Both whisper their unique influential messages into the ear of a person debating an issue. The insight of this illustration is that spiritual and carnal thoughts can exist in the mind unchecked and battling each other. The battle is reducing the carnal and uplifting the spiritual thoughts!

Christians need to prepare for battle. Consider adding the following tools into your spiritual habits.

1. Prioritize study to achieve a deeper understanding of God's word.

Psalm 1:2 connects wisdom with knowing and meditating on God's word. Scripture must reside at the forefront of our minds.

2. Memorize scripture.

Psalm 119:11 encourages hiding the scripture in our hearts so that we will not sin against God. Memorizing scriptures fills our hearts with God's word and when we meditate on them, we are brought closer to spiritual maturity. At the congregation I attend, our ladies bible study class has focused on memorizing scripture for years. We are now taking this a step further by challenging ourselves to memorize entire books of the bible. The purpose is to ensure that scripture and context are ingrained in our thinking, responding, and living.

3. Spend time in fellowship with Christians.

This can be underrated as we contemplate our busy lives, but it can greatly influence whether we skip or slip in our spiritual walk. Building relationships with our brothers and sisters in Christ can mutually enrich and encourage when we allow it. Strive to not be the kind of Christians who walk around dead in our thinking, but ones who live lives rich in the understanding and blessings of Christ.

Questions to Ponder

1. Name examples of how Christians live their lives in a way that could be called spiritually dead?

2. How do Christian standards of success differ from worldly standards?

3. How does the concept of a spiritual filter relate to Mark 7:20-21 and Proverbs 4:23?

4. How can 1 Peter 3:15 help Christians live a life of purpose?

5. Why do you think Christian's struggle with maintaining their spiritual health?

Chapter 2 – The Other gods I Serve

| | | | | | | | | | | | | | | | | | | | | | | | | | | | |

Thinking about the past week, how much of that time did you spend with God whether in formal worship, meditating on scripture, or personal bible study? Only personal reflection can answer the question of how that time compares with all the other stuff we do. If it is embarrassingly low or non-existent, then it is time to figure out if we are serving someone or something other than God.

Serving and Idolatry

According to the Strong's Bible Concordance the word "serve", in both the Hebrew and Greek, refers to cultivating, working, and worshipping. Idolatry is worshipping an idol or cult image which may be a physical image, such as a statue, or a person in place of God.

Combining this understanding about serving and idolatry encourages us to spend time reflecting on what we are cultivating, serving, and worshipping, and whether or not our focus is truly on God or something else. If it is not God, then wherever we are devoting our energy is likely to be the idol that is elevated above God's position.

In Matthew 6:21 there is additional instruction about devotion and where it should be placed.

"For where your treasure is, there your heart will be also."

It clarifies that what is treasured is where the heart will reside. A treasure is what is most valued, protected, or set apart for gifting at a special time. Jewelry, heirlooms, and wealth come to mind when thinking of items that are preserved and passed down through generations. They can have stories, memories, and other special significance attached to them. The point is that these items are important and esteemed in the heart. The scriptural reference to hearts represents our mind and thinking. So, where our mind tends to drift and dwell is our treasure and determines how well we preserve and elevate those treasures.

In summary, what we allow our minds to think about determines what we value. Further, what we value is what we serve and where our precious resources of time, money, and efforts are devoted.

You Shall Have No Other Gods Before Me

God is clear in expressing that He expects to hold the primary position in the lives of His children. Remember the second commandment given in Exodus 20:3-6.

> You shall have no other gods before Me. "You shall not make for yourself a carved image—any likeness of anything that is in heaven above, or that is in the earth beneath, or that is in the water under the earth; you shall not bow down to them nor serve them. For I, the LORD your God, am a jealous God, visiting the iniquity of the fathers upon the children to the third and fourth generations of those who hate Me, but showing mercy to thousands, to those who love Me and keep My commandments.

God is certainly worthy of that distinction because He has provided all including the very existence of humanity. New Testament passages also support that idolatry is not what Christians should pursue!

1 Corinthians 10:14 –
> Therefore, my beloved, flee from idolatry.

Galatians 5:19-20 -
> Now the works of the flesh are evident, which are adultery, fornication, uncleanness, lewdness, idolatry, sorcery, hatred, contentions, jealousies, outbursts of wrath, selfish ambitions, dissensions, heresies,…

When we neglect our responsibility to elevate God in all aspects of our lives, we are giving Satan the preeminence that belongs to God and defying the instruction of James that we resist Satan.

James 4:7 -
> Therefore submit to God. Resist the devil and he will flee from you.

As mentioned previously about the family heirlooms, we may set them apart from our other possessions and save them in a special place. Just like those special items are set apart, God is to be sanctified and set apart in our hearts.

1 Peter 3:15
> *"But sanctify the Lord God in your hearts, and always be ready to give a defense to everyone who asks you a reason for the hope that is in you, with meekness and fear;"*

Sanctifying God in our hearts is acknowledgement that He is our hope, and thus less likely to be deprioritized. There will be a desire to build a personal relationship with Him through studying His Word and praying to Him. As we learn more about what He stands for and His wisdom is put into practice, then our lives begin to change. It may seem like a little change at first, but when we are deliberate in putting His wisdom into practice daily, the impact is evident! His value increases as His wisdom becomes more evident in our character. It will feel out of balance and strange when we miss worship or personal time of study or prayer. Our only response is to recommit and get back on track.

Examples of Idolatry in Old Testament

There are many rich examples of how Israel's idol worship displeased God.

Impatience Leading to Idol Worship

In Exodus 32:1-9, the scene of elation and expectation is seen after Israel experienced the miracle of God's love in their crossing of the Red Sea. However, while Moses was up on Mt. Sinai receiving instructions from God, Israel grew impatient in their waiting and resorted to their old ways as is best displayed in their creating a golden calf to worship. God was very displeased and in verse 8 He said,

> *"They have turned aside quickly out of the way which I commanded them. They have made themselves a molded calf, and worshiped it and sacrificed to it, and said, 'This is your god, O Israel, that brought you out of the land of Egypt!'"*

They actually had the audacity to give the calf credit for all God had done for them! The outcome of this disobedience is shared in verse 35 when the Lord smote the people for their **sin**.

Convenience Leading to Idol Worship

In 1 Kings 12, after the kingdom was divided, King Jeroboam set up worship outside of Jerusalem (vs. 29). King Jeroboam did this out of fear (vs. 26-27) that the 10 tribes would grow weary of traveling to Jerusalem for worship and would eventually stay there, causing Jeroboam to lose his kingdom. His plan was to make it convenient for them to worship in an area geographically closer to them, Bethel and Dan, but very distant from God's will.

Desire for Worldliness Leads to Idol Worship

The prophet Hosea's married life exemplified the disobedience and need for redemption of Israel. Like Hosea's wife, Israel would pursue immorality, receive punishment, but then access restoration through God's mercy in the end. In Hosea 8, Israel is admonished for their idol worship and then told they would pay for it!

Israel Warns Today's Christians

Further in 1 Corinthians 10:1-7, Israel's idolatry and lusting after evil things noted as a warning to New Testament Christians.

> *Moreover, brethren, I do not want you to be unaware that all our fathers were under the cloud, all passed through the sea, all were baptized into Moses in the cloud and in the sea, all ate the same spiritual food, and all drank the same spiritual drink. For they drank of that spiritual Rock that followed them, and that Rock was Christ. But with most of them God was not well pleased, for their bodies were scattered in the wilderness. Now these things became our examples, to the intent that we should not lust after evil things as they also lusted. And do not become idolaters as were some of them. As it is written, "The people sat down to eat and drink, and rose up to play."*

While Israel had partaken in the spiritual things (eaten of the spiritual food and drink), they were still disobedient, and this did not please God. It is significant that their idolatry was specifically called out! When their faith should have been solidly placed in God, they chose to participate in idolatry and were punished for it.

Who is my Master?

God knows we have responsibilities, hobbies of interests, and dreams, but when doing these activities is more important than establishing time for Him, there is an issue. It is the tempting to elevate and make those other things most important that causes trouble. Even when busy with children, husband, jobs, extended family, friends, etc., etc., etc., we do it so much better when we make time for daily devotion and prayer. Some talk about getting up 15 minutes early just to get that time in. It is a gratifying way to start the day and show God He is first in our lives!

James 1 says that temptation comes from one's own desires, which acknowledges that each of us is unique in what we want and what we want to serve. It is certainly not wrong to own possessions, but when our desire for material things, affection, ideology, or notoriety is so critical that we focus more on planning how to achieve and keep those - while forgetting our commitment to God, then our desires need to be checked!

Where Do Idols Come From

A careful review of our minds will reveal what we treasure and thus desire more than God.

Men make objects from that which they are captivated and motivated. This is another way of saying that what we serve is valued and this value has been learned in some way other than bible study. Consider the words of the psalmist in Psalms 135:15-18.

> *The idols of the nations are silver and gold, The work of men's hands.*
> *They have mouths, but they do not speak; Eyes they have, but they do not see;*
> *They have ears, but they do not hear; Nor is there any breath in their mouths.*
> *Those who make them are like them; So is everyone who trusts in them.*

Silver and gold are what captivate and motivate men. These things are created, shaped, and molded by men. They are objects that cannot speak, see, hear, breathe, and have no power over life. Those who make them – and then worship them - are as spiritually dead as the idols! Their efforts are devoted, loving, and honoring that which cannot love them back.

This could sound ludicrous! Do people really serve things they can make, mold, and shape? Who really does this? Sadly, many, even Christians, define their success and level of happiness by their own created idols. It becomes more important for us to own multiple cars and homes than to increase our financial giving to the Lord's church. Tragically, many Christian youth have been taught this lesson too, either directly or indirectly. They likely do not hear as many messages about glorifying God and allowing his characteristics to separate them from the world but will hear more messages about excelling in education or extra-curricular activities and how to join the right social organizations to build their resumes.

Idol worship can be an attempt to fill an emptiness inside. This can come from our past hurt, discouragement, or disappointment. So, instead of allowing the truths, principles, and encouragement of the Bible heal us and thus, fill the gap in our heart, we substitute it with behaviors and activities that bring glory from the world. While there may be satisfaction for a little while, this is not sustainable for the long term. These substitutions are fleeting and do not have the power to fill the emptiness or heal our broken hearts.

In Isaiah 45:20, the prophet admonishes that idols cannot save. Only by submitting fully to God and allowing Him to repair us can idol worship be overcome.

> *Assemble yourselves and come; Draw near together, You who have escaped from the nations. They have no knowledge, Who carry the wood of their carved image, And pray to a god that cannot save.*

Another example of this is the devotion to completing the "Bucket List" of activities. There was a movie a few years ago that focused on how a dying man spent the last days of his life checking off the list of things he never did during his life. This was his way of leaving the earth fulfilled. While there is nothing wrong with attempting to visit every state in the United States, or parachuting, or traveling the seven seas, pursuing these must not overshadow our pursuit of the love of a lifetime that is received only from a commitment to God! This needs to be on our reexamined reprioritized Bucket List activity.

Removing idols

1 Corinthians 10:7 clearly states that idols are not to be worshipped!

And do not become idolaters as were some of them…

As the old gospel preachers used to say, "if we miss that, we should not be allowed to drive home by ourselves". It is a comical way to state what the insight expressed is easy to understand. It is so easy that anyone can understand it. However, it is often not easy to put it into practice.

How are idols removed?

According to 1 John 5:21 and Colossians 3:5, there is an expectation that idol worship will not be a part of the Christian's life and 1 Corinthians 10:14 encourages us to flee from idolatry!

> *1 John 5:21 - Little children, keep yourselves from idols. Amen.*

> *Colossians 3:5 - Therefore put to death your members which are on the earth: fornication, uncleanness, passion, evil desire, and covetousness, which is idolatry.*

> *1 Corinthians 10:14 - Therefore, my beloved, flee from idolatry.*

Pray.

1 Thessalonians 5:17 encourages us to pray all the time. Prioritizing prayer and making it a part of our everyday lives, can help to also keep our mindset in a spiritual frame of reference. It becomes nearly impossible to desire things more than God when we continually focus on Him.

Delight in God's word.

Psalm 1 encourages us to avoid internalizing the thoughts of the ungodly, but to find delight in the word of God and meditate on it all the time. Think about it constantly and expect to learn new insights about our lives and what we must remove and what to add to be more pleasing to Him.

Check our motivations — Make sure God is Glorified.

Psalm 34:2 teaches us … *"Oh, magnify the LORD with me, And let us exalt His name together…"* Our pursuits should always glorify God!

Give Thanks to God.

According to 1 Thessalonians 5:17 we should always thank God for His presence and influence.

Submit to God.

And finally, James 4:7 teaches us to resist Satan and submit to God. The devil's only ultimate response is to flee from us.

> *Therefore submit to God. Resist the devil and he will flee from you.*

Questions to Ponder

1. Why is it important that Christians understand their treasures as taught in Matthew 6:21?

2. Does God expect to be "the" top priority or "a" top priority in the lives of Christians?

3. Give examples of objects men create that they serve as idols.

4. Why would Christians substitute serving their idols for seeking healing from their hurts from God?

5. What are steps that can be taken to remove our idols?

Chapter 3 - *Is it Worth the Cost?*

Temporary Highs and Lasting Lows

We live in a world today that encourages instant gratification. If you want it, you should have it...do what makes you happy. We become so caught up with self and what we feel we deserve, that we fail to calculate the cost of our decisions. What might feel good today, or in the moment, can have damaging effects and long-term consequences.

Think about the drug, alcohol or sex addict. When engaging in such activity, they often experience an indescribable high that lasts for a matter of seconds, minutes, or maybe hours. This high is so powerful, that nothing else matters in that moment. They are just off somewhere in 'la-la land', numb to reality, in a place they look forward to revisiting again, and again, and again at almost any cost.

These kinds of addictions are often highlighted as being most harmful and detrimental to life and relationships. While this is true, most are incognizant of the fact that sin itself is the most addictive drug out here that affects us all. You don't have to be out on a corner, or in the bar or a nightclub. You could be alone in the privacy of your home with a mind full of foolishness. It all starts with your thoughts, your mind, your heart. *'The heart is deceitful above all things, and desperately wicked; who can know it?' Jeremiah 17:9.* Maybe you don't have an issue with drugs, alcohol, or sex, but how about that vulgar, lying, or gossiping tongue? Or maybe your issue is with pride, greed, or the lack of self-control? Perhaps it's knowing the right thing to do and not doing it. All sin is unrighteousness and one is not accepted above the other in the sight of God. Regardless of my sin or yours, if left unaddressed, it will lead to the same result...death (*Romans 6:23*).

> 'But each one is tempted when he is drawn away by his own desires and enticed. Then, when desire has conceived, it gives birth to sin; and sin, when it is full-grown, brings forth death.' James 1:14-15

Sin comes in many shades and colors, sometimes wrapped in a pretty box hand delivered by Satan himself. It's an addiction that only Jesus can free you from and rehabilitate you through His power.

When a commercial comes on television marketing some drug or medication, everything seems fine until they speed through the long list of possible side effects (ex. may cause headaches, high blood pressure, blood clots, urinary tract infection, stroke, suicidal thoughts, etc). There often appears to be more negative side effects than benefits of the drug itself. You can end up subtracting one issue, and adding on 15 more that requires even more medication. How do you solve a problem by compounding it? Something about that equation just never made sense to me. It affirms how we can become so consumed by an issue that we seek out a quick fix. However, these quick fixes don't provide permanent or lasting solutions. They only numb the problem while creating new ones.

I am reminded of the Israelites when they chose to create new issues by rejecting God as their king by requesting an earthly king. They coveted the earthly kings of other nations and sought a carnal remedy for an issue of the heart. Having an earthly king to represent them may have looked good and exciting from the outside, but they were warned by the prophet Samuel of all the negative side effects in 1 Samuel 8:10-20. This king would:

- Take their sons and appoint them for his own chariots and to be his horsemen, and some will run before his chariots.

- Appoint captains over his thousands and captains over his fifties, and set some to plow his ground and reap his harvest, and some to make his weapons of war and equipment for his chariots.

- Take their daughters to be perfumers, cooks, and bakers.

- Take the best of their fields, their vineyards, and their olive groves, and give them to his servants.

- Take a tenth of their grain and their vintage, and give it to his officers and servants.

- Take their male servants, their female servants, their finest young men, and their donkeys, and put them to his work.

- Take a tenth of their sheep.

Samuel essentially explained to the Israelites how this new king would only take, take, take, take, take... all that they have. He explained how this new kingdom high wouldn't last long and how they would only end up crying out to the Lord with regret. Unfortunately, the people were unwilling to see how their needs were already being met. They refused to see that they had a king unlike any other. They had ruler who wanted to make sure they would both survive and thrive! All they could see was their own vision of this majestic earthly king to be like everyone else. Despite many warnings, their response to Samuel was 'OK, Deal, Sign me up!' They were willing to trade the best of everything to become common, subjecting themselves to man instead of God. This attitude resembles the same response we have when we reject God as King of our lives and covet after someone or something that can only provide artificial temporary highs and lasting lows; things or people who take our joy, peace, stability...ultimately our focus and dependence away from our Lord.

Satan is most certainly a liar (John 8:44). That temporary high will have you justifying your destructive behavior. You may have told yourself:

I can't help it.

Well, at least it's not as bad as other things.

Just this once.

You only live once.

I'm still a work in progress.

God knows my heart.

I'm still a good person overall.

The list goes on and on. You feel in control and convince yourself the route you are taking will be worth it and the alternative isn't as attractive or effective. You think you're winning when you are actually suffering great loss.

While viewing a portion of a crime show, it was interesting to see the actions of those showcased as the 'dumbest criminals'. There was the girl who stole an iPhone and then took selfies with it - which uploaded to the owner's iCloud. Then there was the service station employee who hacked the lotto system and all his family and friends were 'mysteriously" winning the lottery. I thought, why would people risk their FREEDOM over such silly and frivolous things?! But I was reminded how this is no different from the things Christians do every day when we partake of the corrupt vs. divine nature (2 Peter 1:4). Every time I choose a substance, person, relationship or situation that is not aligned with God's will, I put the freedoms of my physical, mental, emotional, and spiritual health at risk. I ultimately put my freedom in Christ at risk. Decisions come with consequences that can result in life altering events. Something that wasn't of concern yesterday can easily become today's reality and change the entire course of your life.

Let's look at Eve for example. The only thing she had to be concerned with was enjoying life with her husband in a beautiful, low maintenance home that came furnished with supplies and food for FREE. The Israelites also enjoyed a life they didn't have to work for:

> *"I have given you a land for which you did not labor, and cities which you did not build, and you dwell in them; you eat of the vineyards and olive groves which you did not plant." Joshua 24:13*

This was a pretty good situation, wouldn't you say? Yet one decision...one very bad decision...changed the course of their lives, our lives, forever (Genesis 3). Sometimes we ignore or show ingratitude toward all our many blessings, and focus on the one thing that we can't have, that which is forbidden. We end up compromising everything for that one thing that will only bring us shame and regret. Adam and Eve suffered a new reality following their disobedience to God by partaking from the Tree of Knowledge of Good and Evil. Yesterday, they were immortal and living it up in the blissfulness of the garden. After one bite of what was expected to provide a supernatural high (ability) (Genesis 3:6), they found themselves separated from God, lost their innocence, lost their home, had to work hard for food, would suffer from childbirth pain, leadership in the home would be challenged, and they would also face death. Was it worth the cost?

Then there is Judas Iscariot...the one who betrayed our Lord Jesus Christ. Judas being one of the 12 disciples was privileged to have a personal relationship with Jesus, a front row seat to observe the teachings and witness the miracles, private lessons, and insight that only those closest to Jesus would be privy to during the time of his ministry. He held a position of trust and got to sit and eat at the same table as the Lord. Yet that wasn't enough. Judas was carried away by greed which led him to betray his master - the one who had loved him and been so good to him. Judas later had buyer's remorse and decided it wasn't worth the cost. He attempted to return the pieces of silver he was given for the betrayal. However, he couldn't undo his mistake and was filled with so much guilt and grief that he couldn't live with himself and ended his life (Matthew 27:3-5). Again, was it worth the cost?

The Aftermath

The aftermath of our poor decisions is often a rude awakening of all the newly created damage caused that could have otherwise been avoided. Our attitude will determine if we willfully become repeat offenders, swallowed in victimhood, of if we courageously face the consequences, being accountable for our actions while seeking change and restoration. There might always be things that we regret, but there is still the opportunity to make better choices to experience better outcomes. If we turn to the Lord and allow Him to order our steps, He will help us heal and properly deal with the guilt and shame that plagues us.

Any behavior that is offensive to God should also be offensive to us and lead us to repentance. Isn't it time for a change? Aren't you sick and tired yet of all the miles traveled on the road that only leads to heartache and destruction? Once we understand the effect our decisions have on our soul's salvation, how it strains our relationship with God and impacts the lives of others, we ought to "bear fruit worthy of repentance" (Matthew 3:8). This means to change! To turn away from the sin which easily besets you. It means to demonstrate new behavior that is consistent with your change of heart. Sometimes we selfishly believe that what we do is our business and it has nothing to do with anyone else. We think our absence and unfaithfulness doesn't affect anyone else. It does. Our sin has the power to discourage others to the point they may lose an already wavering faith. Others may follow your poor example and adopt an attitude of indifference toward the sin in their life. The babies are also watching and woe unto him that causes one of them to stumble. 1 Corinthians 12:26 teaches us if one member suffers, all the members suffer with it. The body must function together in unity to be most effective, and we decide whether we will be a help or a hinderance to the work of the church. Don't allow the mishaps to be for nothing. Although you may have fallen time and time again, don't comfortably roll around in the mess. Get up! Get back up and present yourself a useful servant.

> *For a righteous man may fall seven times*
> *And rise again,*
> *But the wicked shall fall by calamity. Proverbs 24:16*

Consider it a blessing to even have the opportunity to rise again since many have fallen and aren't able to find their way back up or are otherwise faced with some kind of lifelong handicap. When Jesus healed the man at the pool of Bethesda, he told him "See, you have been made well. Sin no more, lest a worse thing come upon you," (John 5:14). Sometimes we play Russian Roulette with our lives and take advantage of God's grace and mercy. We don't always receive the punishment or consequence that we rightfully deserve. We should use these moments as an opportunity to do better since we don't know what day will be the day God's hedge is removed and we feel the impact of the bullet from the gun we ourselves kept loaded. Take heed to the many second chances and warnings if you were fortunate enough to receive them. The Lord has invested so much in you and expects a return on His investment. You could have been eliminated long ago for your sinful nature and essentially for doing nothing but taking up space. But Christ continues to advocate for you, holding back the wrath of God (1 John 2:1-2).

> *He also spoke this parable: "A certain man had a fig tree planted in his vineyard, and he came seeking fruit on it and found none. Then he said to the keeper of his vineyard, 'Look, for three years I have come seeking fruit on this fig tree and find none. Cut it down; why does it use up the ground?' But he answered and said to him, 'Sir, let it alone this year also, until I dig around it and fertilize it. And if it bears fruit, well. But if not, after that you can cut it down.'" Luke 13:6-9*

The problem is that so many of us have become so lukewarm and desensitized to our sinful behavior. Worldliness is justified and glorified instead of condemned. Somewhere along the way, God's people stopped being embarrassed or ashamed of how they falsely represent Christianity. God's people forgot how to blush (Jeremiah 6:15). The moment the sin in our lives no longer convicts us and we forget how to blush, our soul is in a state of danger. Instead of striving to become more like Christ in faith and obedience, we become captivated by the wiles of Satan and conformed to the ways, ideals, and nature of this world (Romans 12:1-2). We seek methods and excuses to have less and less Jesus. We reduce our worship assemblies and neglect to attend bible classes for growth and maturity. We don't want to do more than what's 'required'. Have you reached the peak of your Christianity where there is nothing more you can possibly come to know or understand? It's no wonder how Satan easily walks through the doors of our personal lives and begins supporting our foolish ways of thinking. We become comfortable living our own version of Christianity and neglect the characteristics of true discipleship. *So likewise, whoever of you does not forsake all that he has cannot be My disciple (Luke 14:25-33).*

The law of gravity states that what goes up, must come down. This is the same case when it comes to the object of the carnal highs we engage in. Sin is deceitful. It can be fun, enticing, and pleasurable to the flesh; however, before you know it you've become a strung-out addict and now bowing to a different master. *For when you were slaves of sin, you were free in regard to righteousness. What fruit did you have then in the things of which you are now ashamed? For the end of those things is death (Romans 6:20-21).* There is a saying that "sin will take you farther than you ever expected to go; it will keep you longer than you ever intended to stay; and it will cost you more than you ever expected to pay."

If we think about the outcome of our sinful decisions, it's easy to see how those choices negatively impacted our lives or the lives of others. Maybe you've wasted years of life that could've been devoted in service to the Lord. Perhaps you've damaged your character or ruined your influence. Some damage is irrevocable and you have no choice but to live with the consequences of those decisions. It is often in a state of gloom and despair that we seek that form of aid, relief, and comfort that can only be found in the Lord. We find our religion, reclaim our faith, and turn back to the Lord after we've allowed ourselves to be used and abused by the world. By that time, we've accumulated so much baggage that the Lord never intended for us to carry. Even so, the Lord remains ready and willing to help us detox from all the impurities and dysfunction that's wreaked havoc in our lives.

Breaking Up with Your Dealers

Have you ever paused to assess the kind of people you keep in your life? Are you holding on to relationships that hinder your sobriety and growth? Those that are more harmful than anything else? Some of us keep enablers in our lives who encourage or allow negative or self-destructive behavior. Some keep people around who will make excuses for them and help them feel comfortable with their choices. They keep those around who won't challenge them to change. The comfort zone becomes such an easy and comfortable place no matter how unhealthy and dysfunctional it may be. We love hearing "Nobody is perfect" or "We all have something to work on" or "Don't judge me and my sins, and I won't judge you and yours". If "I can't help it" or "It's not my fault", then I can escape being accountable for my actions.

The comfort zone is a place in which we are in control and will admit only those who will assist in maintaining that zone. No accountability, responsibility or sobering comments are allowed. "Going along is getting along" is the creed. It's been well said that coming out of your comfort zone is tough in the beginning, chaotic in the middle, and wonderful in the end…because in the end, it shows you a whole new world.

"We must do away with the Discernment Oppressing People that Exhaust all efforts to live in His excellence. They deal in discouragement, disparaging remarks, and downright darkness. The D.O.P.E. dealers are dispatched to keep one attached to dysfunction. They whisper subtly to itching ears "That's doing too much", "Don't judge me for sinning differently", "The Bible is ideal, but God knows the deal", to keep you swimming fatally in a puddle of misguided religious zeal, accomplishing nothing godly or real." - Bro. Sabin Johnson

Do you have a D.O.P.E. dealer in your life? One with loose morals who supplies or supports your self-destructive habits? These connections or relationships produce no growth, no change, no transformation, and no maturity. These are essentially the deals you've made with others to help you in your journey toward death.

In order to remain on the straight and narrow path, there is some clean-up that must take place. What would be the point of rehabilitation if we bring all the old and harmful stuff with us?

We must remove these sources of temptation from our lives (Matthew 5:29-30). If we maintain easy access to the same people or resources that lead us to sin, we will easily find ourselves in relapse.

We must empty ourselves of that which has no spiritual benefit and replace it with those things or people who will help us live a better way that's pleasing to God. Satan will always try to convince you that you need more than what Christ is offering, but it is important to recognize this as nothing more than a lie.

The cost of discipleship requires continual dying to self. There is much we must give up for the cause of Christ. However, the value of what is to be gained is greater than anything we might count as a loss. Living for Christ will return far more benefits than the cost of sin. If we were to accurately calculate the cost of our sinful behavior, using God's word as the plumb line, we will find that the wages of sin are still the same - death. There will be no negotiations. Is that the price you are willing to pay to remain in your sinful state?

Thanks be to God that we have a different option. We can make a different choice. We can decide the fate of our soul. If we allow the Lord to be our new supplier of all things good and beneficial, we will find every sacrifice to be worth it during this life and the life thereafter. We will count the many blessings and consider them worth every tear, every heartache, or disappointment we will ever experience.

And whoever does not bear his cross and come after Me cannot be My disciple. For which of you, intending to build a tower, does not sit down first and count the cost, whether he has enough to finish it— Luke 14:27-28

Questions to Ponder

1. What are some of the dangers living in a world where instant gratification is encouraged?

2. What is a biblical and personal example of living on a temporary high that will ultimately result in a lasting low?

3. How might your life and the lives of others be impacted when you compromise your position and responsibilities in Christ?

4. What kind of mindset and action is needed in order to recover from a fall?

5. How might you identify the D.O.P.E. dealers and avoid inviting them in your life?

Chapter 4 - The Sound of the Trumpet

The trumpet is one of the oldest instruments in the world and known for its loud and powerful musical presence. Multiple trumpets can overpower almost any other sound. As such, it's no wonder why the Lord instructed Moses to make trumpets of silver which were to be used for the following purposes: to summon the congregation, to consecrate a fast, for signaling the change of camp, for appointed feasts and days of rejoicing, to be sounded over the sacrifices of burnt and peace offerings, and for sounding alarms in times of war. When the Israelites were being attacked by the adversary, those designated were to sound an alarm with the trumpets to be remembered before the Lord and delivered from their enemies (Numbers 10:1-10). A watchman was appointed to get the people's attention, warning them of potential danger so that they may act accordingly.

> *Again, the word of the LORD came to me, saying, "Son of man, speak to the children of your people, and say to them: 'When I bring the sword upon a land, and the people of the land take a man from their territory and make him their watchman, when he sees the sword coming upon the land, if he blows the trumpet and warns the people, then whoever hears the sound of the trumpet and does not take warning, if the sword comes and takes him away, his blood shall be on his own head. He heard the sound of the trumpet, but did not take warning; his blood shall be upon himself. But he who takes warning will save his life. Ezekiel 33:1-5*

At the sound of the trumpet, every man had a choice whether to take heed or ignore the warning. It was a matter of life and death. One could heed the warning by being attentive and responding accordingly, be it taking cover, falling in line, or drawing weapons to prepare for warfare. Or, one could ignore the call with an attitude of carelessness and indifference, neglecting to take seriously the present danger and approaching threat. Throughout the Bible we read of examples of people being warned by God directly (divine communication) or through dreams, angels, prophets, Christ, and the apostles. God's love for mankind runs so deep that he continually and consistently provided guidance and messages to help sober people up and steer them back in the right direction. *"And the LORD God of their fathers sent warnings to them by His messengers, rising up early and sending them, because He had compassion on His people and on His dwelling place," 2 Chronicles 36:15.*

Warnings of the Past

In the very beginning, God warned Adam not to partake of the Tree of the Knowledge of Good and Evil, and how disobedience of this command would lead to death (Genesis 2:16-17). Adam, being the head of the family, passed such warning on to Eve (Genesis 3:2-3). Unfortunately, Eve still allowed herself to be deceived by Satan and when they partook of the forbidden fruit, sin entered the world, changing life for them and all future generations to come.

Noah was divinely warned of the impending flood during a time when rain was a foreign element (Genesis 6). Yet, he acted in faith, not relying on human wisdom or understanding, but by preparing the ark as instructed which would ultimately save him and his household (Hebrews 11:7). He, being warned, became a preacher of righteousness (2 Peter 2:5) to warn others that they too might be saved from the impending destruction on earth. The Lord was patient and longsuffering during the days of Noah, as He waited for men to heed the warning and repent of their wickedness. However, there is a reason why only Noah's family (eight souls) found salvation in the ark (1 Peter 3:20).

Lot was warned by angels to quickly get his family out of Sodom as the city would soon be destroyed (Genesis 19). The Lord showed mercy when Lot lingered, as the angels took hold of his hand and the hands of his wife and daughters to lead them outside of the city. They received additional warnings not to look behind them and to escape to the mountains. Unfortunately, Lot's wife never made it to a mountain or the nearby city of their escape since she ignored the warning not to look back.

King Abimelech was warned by God in a dream by night that Sarah was another man's wife and if he did not restore her to Abraham, he was indeed a dead man along with all who belonged to him (Genesis 20). Abimelech did not hesitate to correct this error, restoring Sarah back to Abraham and also giving him livestock and servants.

Jonah sounded the trumpet for the people of Nineveh. He preached that the city would be overthrown in 40 days. The people were attentive and responded with belief, fasting, mourning and repentance in hopes that God might relent…and He did (Jonah 3).

God warned king Nebuchadnezzar in a dream and by interpretation through Daniel that unless he repents, acknowledging the Lord's authority and power, he would suffer the fate of the dream (Daniel 4). He'd be driven from his kingdom and be made as a beast of the field. Nebuchadnezzar chose to learn the hard way as he continued to glorify himself instead of the Almighty God. He could have saved himself seven periods of time had he listened and heeded the warning.

God used many different prophets to remind the children of Israel of the Lord their God and to warn them of idolatry and anything that would cause them to be unclean and unholy in the presence of God. He warned them of God's wrath and what would happen if they chose not to repent and return to the Lord. We read of much chastening, destruction, and years of captivity that resulted from the hardened, disobedient, impenitent hearts of Israel.

During his years of ministry, Christ warned mankind of sin, called for repentance and that the kingdom of heaven was near. He warned of the wide and narrow gate, the snares of the devil, the leaven of the Pharisees, false prophets, and many concepts such as repentance, forgiveness, pride, humility, materialism, judgment, etc. His apostles then carried forth His ministry - *"Him we preach, warning every man and teaching every man in all wisdom, that we may present every man perfect in Christ Jesus." Colossians 1:28*

In the above examples, some listened and heeded the Word and others ignored and rejected God, His precepts, and His commandments. Nevertheless, these same warnings are being loudly proclaimed today. If you've ever tried to help someone and teach them things for their own good, you know just how discouraging it can be watching someone do the exact opposite and your sound advice disregarded. To watch someone self-destruct is a hard, unfortunate reality.

> *"To whom shall I speak and give warning, that they may hear? Indeed their ear is uncircumcised, And they cannot give heed. Behold, the word of the LORD is a reproach to them; They have no delight in it." Jeremiah 6:10*

> *"Also, I set watchmen over you, saying, 'Listen to the sound of the trumpet!' But they said, 'We will not listen.'" Jeremiah 6:17*

> *"As for the word that you have spoken to us in the name of the Lord, we will not listen to you!" Jeremiah 44:16*

Wake Up Calls

God loves us so much that He sends messages through his word and his servants to be a guiding light on our path, to sound the alarm when we begin to veer off the road headed in the wrong direction. Some of us might have the 'lane departure' warning feature equipped with our vehicles which is designed to help us avoid accidents due to the drifting or departure of the lane. Sometimes the warning is in the form of a flashing indicator or a beeping sound. Sometimes it's the big red STOP sign or the many red flags that we often choose to ignore. Many times, we hear the trumpet or the beeping, or we see the flashing lights, the stop signs, and all the red flags. We feel the urging and leading of the Holy Spirit and the ringing of the conscience. Yet, we often close our eyes and cover our ears while proceeding toward a path of danger and destruction.

How many times have you been in tight situations that had you on your knees begging and promising God that if He brought you deliverance, you would clean up your act, do better, and would be sure not to place yourself in that same situation again? Some of us have been in very dangerous or compromising situations or have nearly lost our lives being with the wrong people, in the wrong place, at the wrong time, doing the wrong things. These experiences tend to shake and sober us up in the moment and we are so thankful to have escaped perhaps the worst possible scenario. However, how many times after being delivered, did you find yourself in similar situations, breaking those same promises, making light of his grace and mercy? The Lord does not desire his sheep to walk in harm's way, let alone be consumed by the error of our ways. He created us with purpose and knows just how we could be used for his glory.

So often we are acquitted of what our sin deserves, and we are released with a warning or a slap on the wrist. This warning should be treated as another chance, an amazing opportunity to make amends, to get back up and move forward in the right direction…to never look back except to see how far we've come. The Lord is sounding the trumpet as He uses his rod and his staff to rescue, protect, guide, and comfort (Psalms 23). The Lord pokes and prods and often allows people or circumstances to arise in our lives in order to get our attention and direct us back on the right path.

What wake up calls and warnings have you been ignoring? It can be difficult to respond to the alarm when in a deep sleep for a long period of time. We hear the alarm but we press snooze over and over again since we aren't ready to wake up. We've come to delight in our current state and desire to remain just a little while longer. We despise the alarm and its disruption of our comfort as we rest in folly.

Are you still sleeping and resting when you are to be alert, waiting and watching (Mark 14:41)? How many times have you pressed snooze in areas of life where God is trying to wake you up? We tell ourselves we just need "five more minutes", a delay which can easily turn into hours, days or years that you're still lying in your sick bed with no progress or road to recovery. Just a little while longer until I stop drinking, until I stop fornicating, until I change my profane language and company, until I start teaching others, until I start serving in the church, until I start professing and living out my faith. Just a little while longer... *"For we have spent enough of our past lifetime in doing the will of the Gentiles—when we walked in lewdness, lusts, drunkenness, revelries, drinking parties, and abominable idolatries." 1 Peter 4:3.* When God calls, the time to answer is NOW!

Being Prepared

Who is blowing the trumpets today? Preachers of the gospel message along with every person who has obeyed the gospel. Each time we **meditate on God's Word**, this mirror reveals and alerts us to the ugly within that needs to be addressed and transformed. Each time the word of God is proclaimed through God's manservant, we ought to **receive it with gladness** and hear the special message God tailor made just for us for reproof, correction, and instruction in righteousness (2 Timothy 3:16-17).

> *Therefore, lay aside all filthiness and overflow of wickedness, and receive with meekness the implanted word, which is able to save your souls. James 1:21*

We don't take issue with people informing us when we have food on our face, a booger in our nose, or a hole, an unfastened button or zipper on our garments. We respond with gratitude, thankful someone thought enough about us to not allow us to walk around disorderly or unpresentable. We are often even embarrassed when we discover such things on our own after going an entire day looking like who knows what. We take no issue with those warnings that alert us to our physical appearance, safety, or livelihood. However, we tend to tense up, become offended or overwhelmed with negative feelings or emotion when warned about our spiritual condition. We don't even want other Christians knowing our business as not to risk being held accountable for our hypocrisy and unfaithfulness or alerted to our drifting away. We foolishly respond with "no thank you" to those God has put in place to help watch over our souls in order to avoid the snares or dummy traps of Satan (Hebrews 13:17). *"I do not write these things to shame you, but as my beloved children I warn you." I Corinthians 4:14*

Imagine our country being under attack and our troops being unprepared for battle. What if during times of peace, soldiers neglected routine training and discipline... if they had to figure out where they last left their armor and artillery and needed to refamiliarize themselves on proper use of weapons ...if they all entered panic mode when called for battle…? An unprepared and unorganized army will easily lead to chaos and utter defeat. Even when soldiers aren't in battle, they must train and prepare for battle so they can be ready at any given moment.

We are in a spiritual warfare fighting against principalities, powers, rulers, and hosts of darkness and wickedness in heavenly places (Ephesians 6:12). This requires us to use our spiritual senses and weapons:

> *"Therefore, take up the whole armor of God, that you may be able to withstand in the evil day, and having done all, to stand. Stand therefore, having girded your waist with truth, having put on the breastplate of righteousness, and having shod your feet with the preparation of the gospel of peace; above all, taking the shield of faith with which you will be able to quench all the fiery darts of the wicked one. And take the helmet of salvation, and the sword of the Spirit, which is the word of God;" Ephesians 6:13-17*

An estranged relationship with God will cause us to blindly surrender or attempt to enter this battle on our own. Without consistent spiritual training and discipline, we weaken our ability to be on alert and our response time will be greatly delayed. We will miss our orders from the Commander, compromising God's army and becoming more of an asset for the enemy. Although we've been given all the tools necessary to be victorious (the whole armor of God), our level of skill and ability in using and applying these tools will be lacking. A soldier without armor, skill, strategy, troops or leadership is a dead man.

There are certain things in life that we might approach with a "wing it" attitude. According to Merriam-Webster, to wing it is "to do or try to do something without much practice or preparation". Maybe you've winged a presentation or interview before, or maybe an exam or assessment. Perhaps you didn't have time to prepare or simply didn't prioritize preparation, so you just dived in there not really knowing what to expect or how you would answer. Yet, you maintained hope that things would still come together and all would turn out in your favor. We must be careful not to approach Christianity in this same manner if our intentions are to go to Heaven. You may have heard the expression 'Heaven is a prepared place for a prepared people'. Preparation takes place every day we are granted to live. Satan doesn't take breaks or vacations, so we must remain on guard, ready, standing firm with faith saturated in God's Word in order to see, dodge and quench the darts being fired in our direction. When we are hit, we need to have the strength and willpower to get back up and courageously remain in the battle. **We must effectively and strategically use all the armor we've been given to resist the enemy and protect our salvation and the reward awaiting us.**

When the Last Trumpet Sounds...

At the sound of the last trumpet, there will be no more warnings, no more chances, and no more getting ready. Where you stand and who you're standing with on the day of judgment will determine your soul's dwelling place. If we spend our days living for God and in preparation to meet him, the sound of the last trumpet will be received with much jubilance. It will be the most exciting and best day EVER. There will be no fear, regret, or sadness because we can be confident that we will now be freed of this flesh and welcomed into Heaven to be eternally with our Lord.

> "Behold, I tell you a mystery: We shall not all sleep, but we shall all be changed— in a moment, in the twinkling of an eye, at the last trumpet. For the trumpet will sound, and the dead will be raised incorruptible, and we shall be changed." 1 Corinthians 15:51-52

> "For the Lord Himself will descend from heaven with a shout, with the voice of an archangel, and with the trumpet of God. And the dead in Christ will rise first. Then we who are alive and remain shall be caught up together with them in the clouds to meet the Lord in the air. And thus, we shall always be with the Lord."
> 1 Thessalonians 4:16-17

The sound of the last trumpet will only result in panic or sorrow if we are unprepared. If you weren't sober then, this will definitely be an event that will wake you up. Maybe you can recall the pop quizzes teachers often distributed during class. If you haven't learned and studied the material or given it any thought for that matter, the pop quiz might come as a disappointing shock to which you've already accepted the high probability of failure. You begin thinking about how this score could affect your entire grade, how much time or how many assignments are left in the semester or if there's any extra credit available to help balance out your scores.

This extra stress or train of thought is often preventable especially if the teacher warned there would be quizzes throughout your time in this class. Even if the date was not provided, having the understanding that a quiz could occur at any given time should lead to a state of readiness. We don't know when the Lord will return, but we can still live in a state of expectation, knowing that He surely will return and at a time we might least expect it (1 Thessalonians 5:2). He provided the warning and was gracious enough to instruct us on how to prepare for this day. At the sound of the trumpet, will you be ready?

Questions to Ponder

1. What were some of the purposes for the trumpet to be sounded during biblical times?

2. What was each person's responsibility regarding the sounding of the trumpet?

3. Discuss examples of different warnings provided throughout scripture and the response to such warnings. What can be learned from these examples?

4. What warnings and wake up calls might you be ignoring in your life where God could be trying to get your attention?

5. How might one remain alert and in a state of readiness and preparation?

Chapter 5 - Stop with the Excuses!

"Too many are too willing to rationalize away accountability, and that obstructs behavior change."

~Ross Tucker

Excuses are what we use to justify our secret refusal to do something that we find unnecessary or undesirable. We use them to rationalize away any potential consequences of that decision. Such a habit will cause one to miss out on many growth opportunities. When seeking to be released or exempted from an obligation or duty, we often spend more time and energy trying to find an excuse than it would have taken to just simply do what has been asked or expected of us.

We intentionally look for excuses. If you've spent a lot of time around children, you've definitely been exposed to how easy and often excuses may occur. Children can come up with excuses for just about anything and everything. There's an excuse as to why they got in trouble in class, why they haven't completed their chores, why they missed their curfew, and why it's everyone's fault but their own. Adults alike often find and use just as many excuses to shift the blame or responsibility or to hide true motives and intent.

Excuses are even packed and loaded for use at our discretion and convenience with just a simple internet search. We don't even have to be creative anymore. Google will provide suggestions for just about any excuse you are in need of…it's ready and available right at your fingertips. Unfortunately, excuses have greatly gained more popularity than honesty and accountability. They are also often disguised as 'reasons', but these are not one in the same. There will be valid reasons and circumstances that play a role in an outcome or behavior. However, reasons become excuses when they are used to avoid responsibility. For example, someone might offer the following reasons for not serving in the church:

- I wasn't asked to do anything.
- They already know who they want serving in those areas.
- I work better alone than with other people.
- I already have enough responsibilities in my personal life.

These reasons are being used to avoid responsibility; therefore, making them excuses. Could you take some initiative instead of waiting to be asked? Are you being presumptuous as to who is needed or what would be helpful? Are you unwilling to put forth effort in working effectively with others? Is the Lord's work not important enough to make a priority in your life? It's easy to come up with excuses as to why our spiritual growth is stunted, why we can't serve when called, why we don't pray or study as we should, why we've isolated ourselves from the body of Christ, why we don't share God's word with others, and so forth. **Maturity calls us to be accountable, take responsibility, and look for reasons to do and be better** (John 15:22; Acts 17:30; Romans 1:20-21; James 4:17).

Adam and Eve

We find the first use of excuses in the account of Adam and Eve after they sinned in the Garden of Eden (Genesis 3:9-13). When confronted by God, they had the opportunity to confess and be accountable for the sin they committed. However, there was quite a bit of blame shifting that took place:

> *Then the Lord God called to Adam and said to him, "Where are you?" So he said, "I heard Your voice in the garden, and I was afraid because I was naked; and I hid myself." And He said, "Who told you that you were naked? Have you eaten from the tree of which I commanded you that you should not eat?" Then the man said, "The woman whom You gave to be with me, she gave me of the tree, and I ate." And the Lord God said to the woman, "What is this you have done?" The woman said, "The serpent deceived me, and I ate."*

Adam places blame on the woman God gave to him. However, it was Adam who received the commandment directly from the Lord not to eat of the tree of the knowledge of good and evil (Genesis 2:15-17). It was Adam whom God made head of his wife and family, therefore, responsible for teaching Eve all that God commanded. It was Adam who was there with Eve when she took of the forbidden fruit, eating right along with her. It was also Adam whom God called as they attempted to hide themselves from the presence of the Lord.

Eve then blames the serpent for deceiving her. However, it was Eve who received the command of God through Adam as to which tree they were not to eat from. It was Eve who entertained conversation with the crafty serpent and allowed her mind to be open to strange teaching. It was also Eve's lust and pride that led her to be enticed and deceived by the desires of her heart (James 1:14-15; 1 John 2:16).

Moses

God called Moses to lead His people out of Egypt and bring them to the land they were to inherit. However, Moses saw nothing but problems with this plan while offering the following excuses (Exodus 3-4):

- *"Who am I that I should go to Pharaoh, and that I should bring the children of Israel out of Egypt?"*

- *"But suppose they will not believe me or listen to my voice; suppose they say, 'The Lord has not appeared to you.'"*

- *"O my Lord, I am not eloquent, neither before nor since You have spoken to Your servant; but I am slow of speech and slow of tongue."*

- *"O my Lord, please send by the hand of whomever else You may send."*

Who are you Moses? Absolutely nobody…that is nobody without the Lord. Moses was so focused on what he perceived to be his limitations or inadequacies that he didn't consider who was calling him to lead in the first place. Perhaps you're familiar with the expression, "God doesn't call the qualified, He qualifies the called." God would not ask us to do anything without preparing and equipping us with the necessary tools to accomplish the task. It's true that Moses could not lead and speak on behalf of this great nation on his own. The hand of the Lord would be the reason behind his success should he not allow excuses to hinder him.

The Great Supper

In The Parable of the Great Supper, we learn of a man who invited many people to a great feast he was hosting (Luke 14:15-24). However, once the supper was prepared and ready and the guests were called, this invitation was rejected and only met with excuse after excuse:

- *"I have bought a piece of ground, and I must go and see it. I ask you to have me excused."*

- *"I have bought five yoke of oxen, and I am going to test them. I ask you to have me excused."*

- *"I have married a wife, and therefore I cannot come."*

The host wasn't asking for much; in fact, he was showing much generosity and hospitality. The only thing required of those invited was to come and enjoy the provisions. Yet still, some did not desire to give such event and opportunity the time of day. We offer similar excuses that cause us to miss out on a great meal and sweet fellowship. Sometimes the children are the excuse or the job we accepted where we allowed working on Sundays to be an option. Other times we are too tired or we cough one time and now we're too sick to attend. When we avoid communion with the One who blesses us with time and opportunity, and who offers us salvation, we begin to despise and trade our birthright of Heaven.

There are many biblical examples of people using excuses to avoid responsibility and ignore the will of God. It is important that we also examine ourselves to determine if excuses have hindered our growth and service to the Lord…

The Constant Victim

The Constant Victim makes excuses, rationalizes, and blames others for their choices, mistakes, regression, or whenever they are feeling slighted. They refuse to accept responsibility and are the first to point the finger toward everything and everyone but themselves. It's usually someone else's fault as to why they feel how they feel, why they said what they said, and why they do what they do. The truth is, we all have a choice, and we often choose to do the things we find ourselves involved with (James 1:14). Someone else's action or desire can't cause us to do wrong. The wrong results from what already resides within the heart.

How many people have you known to disappear from congregations, either falling away from the church completely or withdrawing fellowship or church membership? There are many who become offended and depart on bad terms, neglecting to face challenges, conflict, or rebuke with the spirit of Christ. It seems we are willing to be uncomfortable and endure challenges in the workplace, within our homes, in our worldly friendships and relationships… everywhere except for God's church. The moment we are in disagreement, feelings are hurt or toes get stepped on, we adopt a series of 'they' 'they' 'they' and we are ready to walk away. If it's that easy to walk away, it may be because we weren't truly invested in the first place. Growth results from perseverance, not by running in the face of conflict or church hopping every time the leadership "makes you" upset. The Lord has provided guidance on how to handle these matters (Matthew 18:15-17), and we must be sure to do our part in self-examination.

Remaining in a state of victimhood keeps you trapped in time as you replay offenses in your mind over and over again. Seeds of bitterness and resentment begin to sprout and relationships are severed. While there will be times we are legitimately wronged and circumstances where appropriate to walk away, we can trust God to bring about peace and comfort (Psalm 147:3). The past does not have to overplay its role in our present and future lives and relationships. Instead of being a victim, we can choose to be victorious in Christ.

The Work in Progress

There are some who often excuse their ungodly behaviors with the disclaimer of being a 'work in progress'. Any new creature in Christ certainly can be a work in progress. However, one must actively work toward progression. When we compare our yesterdays to where we are today in the Lord, a significant difference ought to be apparent. We should have an extensive list of 'I used to(s) but now' to see all the ways we were walking according to the flesh, but now how we are walking according to the Spirit. This will naturally occur as we submit to God's will and allow the transformation process to take place (Romans 12:2). Unlike man, God never starts something that He is unable to finish. He desires to work in and through us until He calls us to rest.

> "...being confident of this very thing, that He who has begun a good work in you will complete it until the day of Jesus Christ;"

The Lord is always at work and committed to the process of our growth and development. He causes the increase (1 Corinthians 3:6), but the seed only grows where there is good soil, within a noble and good heart (Luke 8:15). Sometimes we drag out the growth process on a weaning plan for 10 to 20 years, when there are many activities and behaviors we can simply decide to stop doing today and never look back from this point on. The problem is that we don't want to give up these things.

When Paul addressed the Philippian church, he made note that although he has come a mighty long way from who he used to be, he still has a long way to go. He acknowledges he still has weaknesses and flaws, but he does not remain stagnant. He presses on, reaches forward, and presses toward his spiritual goals and allows God to perfect him.

> *"Not that I have already attained, or am already perfected; but I press on, that I may lay hold of that for which Christ Jesus has also laid hold of me. Brethren, I do not count myself to have apprehended; but one thing I do, forgetting those things which are behind and reaching forward to those things which are ahead, I press toward the goal for the prize of the upward call of God in Christ Jesus."*

We too must work, pressing and reaching forward to our higher calling. Otherwise, our spiritual goals will never be realized. No work, no progress. "He's not done with me yet" may be a true statement but we should also consider if our actions, or lack thereof, are indicators of us being done with Him.

///////////////////////////////

I'm Only Human

"For He knows our frame; He remembers that we are dust."

Closely related to the work in progress, is its companion excuse of "I'm only human". This is when we make excuses for doing things that displease the Lord claiming to be only human – "I can't help it, and that's okay. God knows I'm just a man or a woman with my share of faults and weakness." While it's good and acceptable to recognize our human limitations, there is danger in concluding that we can never overcome challenges or develop into anything more than we are today. Yes, we all have our weaknesses. Yes, we all may stumble at times. Yes, it's an already known fact that we are an imperfect people. However, if we stop right there, where's the hope and the victory? Let's not forget we are perfectible, we are more than conquerors, and we are victorious with the help of our Lord.

When God our Creator formed man, there was no confusion regarding man's substance. We have a physical body (flesh), a spirit which animates us and an immortal soul. Although physically made of dust, we were also created in His image with a spiritual personality and moral likeness (Genesis 1:26, 2:7). The Lord knows exactly what we're made of and what we're capable of accomplishing. We have much more to offer than our human nature.

> *"Your eyes saw my substance, being yet unformed. And in Your book they all were written, The days fashioned for me, When as yet there were none of them."*

> *"Before I formed you in the womb I knew you; Before you were born I sanctified you; I ordained you a prophet to the nations."*

The Lord made us with a distinct purpose. He knows who we are and what we are destined to become. Some conclude that God's expectations are unrealistic and unattainable, so why even bother trying. This disposition is flawed in that while we are human, we are not 'only human' nor should we be striving to be more human than spiritual. Jesus didn't die on the cross for us to remain "only human". We didn't receive the gift of the Holy Spirit to remain only human. We were set free from sin in order to become slaves to righteousness. The whole point is to no longer be a slave to the flesh and to sin, but to be righteous and alive in God.

> *"For I delight in the law of God according to the inward man. But I see another law in my members, warring against the law of my mind, and bringing me into captivity to the law of sin which is in my members. O wretched man that I am! Who will deliver me from this body of death? I thank God—through Jesus Christ our Lord! So then, with the mind I myself serve the law of God, but with the flesh the law of sin."*

Without the Lord's presence and working in our lives, we are powerless and will easily succumb to the works of the flesh. I truly am only human Without Him and will lose as the flesh wars against the spirit. It is through Christ who strengthens me, that I am able to win (Philippians 4:13).

God knows my heart

One attribute of God is that He is Omniscient. This means He is an all-knowing God. He knows and is aware of EVERYTHING, including the nature of one's heart. Sometimes our actions or efforts may be misunderstood by others, and we take comfort in the fact the Lord knows our true motive and intent. He is a witness that in such moments we were coming from a pure and genuine place. It is also comforting to know that in those moments of failure, when we fall short of God's glory, that He knows our true heart's desire is to serve and please him. God should find remorse and penitence in the hearts of those who love him.

"God knows my heart" is a dangerous excuse since this very fact should cause us to fear the upkeep of any form of evil or deceit dwelling within. God knows when we choose our self-interest over Him and others. He knows when we are capable of doing something but make little or no effort. He knows what and who has priority in our lives. We may lie and put on a good front for others, but the Lord is the one person who can easily see right through us and expose us for the frauds that we are.

"The heart is deceitful above all things, And desperately wicked; Who can know it? I, the Lord, search the heart, I test the mind, Even to give every man according to his ways, According to the fruit of his doings." Jeremiah 17:9-10

Ananias and Sapphira learned this lesson the hard way when they lied to the Holy Spirit (Acts 5:1-11). The church was newly established, growing rapidly, and believers were sharing in all things for the common good. Many were selling their property and bringing all the proceeds to the apostles to distribute to any one in need. Ananias and Sapphira got caught up in appearances and wanted others to think they turned over all the money from the sale of their possession, when they actually held back a portion for themselves. They were in a position to give whatever they wished at their discretion. They were also in a position to simply be truthful regarding their contribution amount. Unfortunately, they conceived hypocrisy and deceit in their hearts, lying to men and to God. A decision that cost them their lives.

A consistent prayer should be our request for God to reveal any form of unrighteousness in our hearts… to bring these things to our attention so that we may have a pure and clean conscience and not suffer the same fate of death.

"Search me, O God, and know my heart; Try me, and know my anxieties; And see if there is any wicked way in me, And lead me in the way everlasting."

Worship is Boring

And let us consider one another in order to stir up love and good works, not forsaking the assembling of ourselves together, as is the manner of some, but exhorting one another, and so much the more as you see the Day approaching. Hebrews 10:24-25

Many of us forsake the assembling of ourselves or get nothing out of worship since we find the services to be boring, antiquated or irrelevant. We grow weary of sitting for hours singing the same old songs and hearing the same old lectures. We find different things to complain about or people to criticize. We might even find ourselves scrolling on Facebook, browsing the internet, texting… any distraction is welcomed to help us escape this 'dry' experience which has become nothing more than ritualistic. It is now common to see children on the pews with tablets on their laps and headphones over their ears, as they play their games and engage in other activities. Think about it… in the house of the Lord where God's Word is being proclaimed, we've covered our children's ears with the excuse that they'll only be a distraction or they won't be able to understand or be attentive anyway. Some of us even leave them at home as if their presence is without purpose or benefit (Matthew 19:14).

We use human reasoning to make excuses for not attending Bible classes or services, acting as judge of what is deemed necessary, required, or profitable. However, we should desire to worship not out of obligation, but out of necessity with a desire to satisfy our spiritual appetite and responsibilities as servants of the Lord. If we aren't getting anything out of it, we should consider what we are putting in… If God is truly the object of our worship, the focus will be on pleasing him and not ourselves. For worship is not for our personal entertainment, but to honor our Lord and render obeisance to him alone. We are to worship him in spirit and in truth (John 4:24), with prepared minds and open mouths ready to receive the meal prepared just for us. Why search for reasons not to attend when it's for your edification and the edification of others? If anything, we should welcome and eagerly await any opportunity to learn more about our God and his will for our lives. Excuses regarding the requirements, distance, timeframe, lessons, members, etc. will only result in harm to our spiritual growth and development.

No More Excuses

We must stop making excuses for ourselves and for others and instead challenge one another to be more faithful and useful servants in the kingdom. Sometimes we make excuses for family or friends who won't obey and often spend a great deal of time trying to change or convince a person who has no desire for truth or change. However, you cannot make a blind man see. We can't expect others to change just because we have. We can only exemplify Christ and be a source of encouragement. At the end of the day, either we believe in him and what He said or we don't, either we're willing to follow him or we're not, either we desire growth and relationship with him and the family of Christ, or we don't. So, let's stop enabling bad habits and considering ourselves to be more compassionate and understanding than God. Let's stop looking for loopholes or creating grey areas that don't exist in order to serve our own purpose. Let's acknowledge all the reasons He has given us to do more, to think higher, to love harder, and to be greater in the new man created and renewed according to God in true righteousness and holiness (Ephesians 4:24; Colossians 3:10).

Questions to Ponder

1. What is the difference between an excuse and a reason?

2. In what ways will excuses hinder your growth, development, and relationships?

3. What are some biblical examples of those who offered excuses when called to service or when confronted for a wrong doing?

4. Why would it be advantageous to seek and find the many reasons to become a better servant vs. looking for excuses to remain stagnant?

5. What are some areas in your life where you need to stop making excuses and instead accept challenges, responsibility and accountability?

Chapter 6 - Accepting God's Will

The biggest challenge that is necessary in accepting God's will is getting over ourselves in order to get out of his way. Humility is key! Luke 9:23 says, *"if anyone desires to come after Me, let him deny himself, and take up his cross daily, and follow Me."* When we made the decision to become a Christian, we chose to follow Jesus. This involves following his example and his pattern in all we do. Yes, that includes keeping our thoughts and desires in line with his thoughts, desires and plans for us. When we humble ourselves, we are allowing room for his guidance. *"The humble He guides in justice, And the humble He teaches His way"* (Psalm 25:9-10). That means He is guiding us in the right (just) way. We are allowing him to guide and to teach. There are probably many times we can look back at decisions we made based upon our feelings, goals, and desires. Humility opens the door to admitting that we were wrong and that we went about things our way and not his. We did not deny ourselves the opportunity to act upon what we wanted. We went ALL in on what WE desired. Christ humbled himself by denying his will. He asked for the cup to be passed from him, but ultimately knew the cost of sin was separation from the Father. Nonetheless, as Matthew 26:42 says *"O My Father, if this cup cannot pass away from Me unless I drink it, Your will be done."* He accepted the Father's will and was obedient to it by taking on our sin. That was a huge load to bear. He denied himself of his will to not be separated from the Father. He chose to become sin so that we could be free from spiritual death and be forgiven of our sins. If we put that into perspective, things start becoming clear. With clarity we can be honest with ourselves, sober minded and admit that we are acting upon our will. We have not denied ourselves or sacrificed our will. We do not make the best decisions or choices in life when we leave God out. We should be consulting Him in prayer and weighing our thoughts with his through his revealed word. We, like Jesus, have to deny ourselves in order to be like him. *"My food is to do the will of Him who sent me, and to finish it."* John 4:34.

Learning to accept Gods' will takes a willingness to accept what is NOT in our control. Learning that which sustains me when I am carrying out his will is in his word and His promises to us. He promises that He would provide for us, protect us, and avenge us. His daily display of this is what continues to fuel us to keep keeping on. We made it through those days only with his help, and only with what He provided. There is nothing we have done that has been truly defined as good (according to his definition) because of our say so, but it is because the Lord has said so. Looking at the beginning of the Serenity Prayer, it says, "God grant me the serenity to accept the things I cannot change, the courage to change the things I can and the wisdom to know the difference." There are many things that we can control. The biggest is the ability to control our decision-making process. God gives us free moral agency to make decisions on our own and to choose the path we take. We can choose to take the spiritual path that He has graciously offered us through his son or the carnal one which is the way of Satan, the prince of the air. However, his desire is for us to make our decisions based on his will and purpose for our lives. That can be a daunting task to many. It becomes daunting because it becomes a battle of his will and ours. Unfortunately, as the saying goes "the heart wants what it wants." Romans 12 describes this battle beautifully. Carnal thinking gets carried away and caught up in thinking as the world thinks. For instance, when we are deciding if a personal relationship with the opposite sex is something we ought to pursue, we may get caught up in the world's standards. We will seek to answer questions such as: "Does he or she have a good job? Am I physically attracted to him/her? Are they in shape physically? Do they have the same sense of style?" However, when we stop, think, and examine ourselves (2 Corinthians 13:5), we can see they are not spiritual thoughts at all and do not exhibit Christ in us. As Christians, when we are unified in the mind of Christ, we will be spiritually minded. Not one of these thoughts is going to help achieve any level of spiritual maturity, and wake us up to the "sin that so easily beset us" (Hebrews 12:1) or help us to be sober minded. They are, however, common thoughts of a carnal mind. We may easily hear these phrases from co-workers, or friends and family that are of the world and even ourselves when we are letting the carnal side peak its ugly head. Such thoughts or phrases should not be as easy or common to hear coming from a Christian. When we chose to repent, wake up and turn from that sinful path, we decided to change our thoughts and follow Christ's way. We made the conscious decision to let the Spirit, that now dwells in us from the time we were baptized, to guide us into righteousness. That being the case, there should be no problem accepting his will. Otherwise, we are grieving the Spirit (Ephesians 4:30). At the point of baptism, we have made it our business to trust in him so much that we are willing to accept all that is in his will. The first being to turn away from our will.

Self-examination is a part of his will for us as well as a command (2 Corinthians 13:5). We must do it. If these carnal thoughts are ours, we have a duty to figure out why we are thinking this way. Any time our thoughts are not spiritual, self-examination needs to take place. If it does not, we are not being spiritually minded, but are carnal minded. God knows exactly what we need to be more like Christ. He knows our thoughts and intentions and only his Spirit can properly guide us.

"For what man knows the things of a man except the spirit of the man which is in him? Even so no one knows the things of God except the Spirit of God. Now we have received, not the spirit of the world, but the Spirit who is from God, that we might know the things that have been freely given to us by God. These things we also speak, not in words which man's wisdom teaches but which the Holy Spirit teaches, comparing spiritual things with spiritual." (1 Corinthians 2:11-13)

It was his gift to us…why wouldn't we use it? In these Scriptures we learn that carnal thinking is not at all included in his will for us at any time, so it would absolutely be going against his will when choosing a mate or when choosing any type of relationship based on those thoughts. If we are being spiritual, we accept that in every single decision we should be consulting his will. After accepting that, then the following questions will be easier to answer: Are we choosing a spiritual companion or are we just choosing someone because others have taken that path? Are we really ready for a mate? Why am I not consulting the Lord's will on this matter? Do I already know the Lord's will? Why have I not accepted what I know his will to be? As mentioned earlier, examination of self is necessary. God makes it easy for us to know his will. What becomes the challenge is accepting it. Perhaps another explanation why accepting it is challenging is because we are attempting to play God or better put…be a god. Part of his will is for us to allow *"His word to richly dwell within us."* (Colossians 3:16). When we allow that to happen, we are walking in the Spirit. We are allowing him to direct our path. Walking in the Spirit involves being patient in the Lord, waiting for his answer, not rushing into situations which brings destruction because it is walking in the flesh (Galatians 5:16). Once we are walking spiritually, accepting God's will is automatic because of the faith and trust we have in him, "we *live by every word that proceedeth from his mouth*" (Matthew 4:4). We then have the wisdom to realize and accept that The Father knows best.

|||||||||||||||||||||||||||||||

Father Knows Best

The show "Father Knows Best" comes to mind when I hear this phrase. No, I am not dating myself, I was actually not born when this came out. However, I am a fan of old TV shows. I remember that this show was based around the fact that, indeed, the father knew what was best for the family. It seems a simple concept since why wouldn't the father, the protector, the provider, the guider know all the right things to say and all the right advice to give? Times have certainly changed from when this show came out. We now live in a world that has very little regard for fathers. They are actively trying to omit fathers from the family.

Most TV shows today are centered around how messy fathers are and all the chaos they have created. They do their best to try to disparage the father instead of holding him in high regard. For the Christian, we know that fathers are still vital to the family, the church, and society. First, because our Heavenly Father told us they are. In Genesis 2:24 the word father first appears. In this text, the Hebrew word for father is AB, meaning Chief/principal…the head of, first in position, or the leader. The TV show showed us the ideal image of an earthly father, but also has principles that we could gain from a spiritual aspect. In the show, the father is the head, and solves everyone's issues. Everyone seeks him. That is what God our Heavenly Father wants from us as his children. It is evident all around us in this chaotic world that godly fathers are needed. Unfortunately, the perspective on the TV show, of the earthly father being the ultimate source of wisdom, still tends to be more accepted than the simple truth that our godly Father ultimately knows best and holds all the wisdom. That is because acknowledging the godly part would hold folks accountable for their lack of submission to his will. For this reason, shows have gone so far away from the topic of fatherhood. God our Father knows what's best for us because He created us. He created us for his purpose. Too often, it seems we forget this, therefore the connection of him knowing what is best for us gets lost. He gave us a pattern to follow. He wants earthly fathers to follow HIS pattern. He wants fathers to be godly and to lead their families. He also wants the families to look to the Heavenly Father for guidance. When the earthly father follows the lead of the Heavenly Father, he will submit to his will as an example of submission to the family. He will continue to remind and point all to God the Father, making him a godly father.

    The Lord's plans for us are far greater than we could ever imagine (Ephesians 3:20). We often think up these grandiose ideas and thoughts of what we think is best, but even our biggest thoughts and ideas are nowhere close to what God has planned for us. Perhaps we forget what it says in Isaiah 55:8-9, *"For my thoughts are not your thoughts. Your ways are not my ways declares the Lord. For as the Heavens are higher than the Earth, so are my thoughts higher than your thoughts."* This scripture tells us that there will be things we don't understand, as to the whys, the hows and such. Therefore, we must accept and trust He always has what is best for us in mind. He makes no mistakes, and when we truly believe that, we will be more than willing to accept his will. When we assess our decisions next to his and consider the times we have chosen to accept God's will for us while allowing his process to unfold, we will see how his results are better than ours. God's results will always be better than anything we have planned even when it isn't very comfortable. When we decide to stop thinking we have made all the best decisions, as if we have done anything on our own….as if we are God, the path that He has set forth becomes more and more clear. We are able to free our minds of the tainted views, perceptions, lies, and assumptions we keep deceiving ourselves with over and over. After getting past these negative thoughts and mindsets we can then allow the Lord to work more perfectly in us. *"Letting our hearts be perfect with the Lord our God, to walk in his statutes, and to keep his commandments, as at this day"* (1Kings 8:61). Prayerfully, we can truly acknowledge that we need Him, that we can do nothing without Him, and that we only cause harm to ourselves when we put our trust in ourselves. The apostle Paul told the jailer, "Do thyself no harm" (Acts 16:28) which is meant for us today as well. God is rebuking us and telling us to not let our thoughts go astray for it will only cause harm leading to destruction. Acknowledging these things will allow his good and perfect will to prevail in our lives. Living the Christian life means that we have matured into the understanding that the Father knows best. We have awoken and stopped doing harm to ourselves by ignoring the Father's wisdom. We are now sober and fully aware in spirituality instead of drunk on carnality. We are ready to accept all that He has in store for us…even when we don't get the answers we want.

|||||||||||||||||||||||||||||||

Yes, No, Not Right Now

When we pray, God always hears us (1 John 5:14). There are times we may feel that our prayers are not being answered. Prayer should come with faith. Faith and trust that we are being heard and with the full assurance and confidence that whatever the answer is, it was the best answer because it came from the Father. He knows all the ins and outs of every situation, from past, present, and future. The fact that He is omniscient, omnipotent and omnipresent can be forgotten. He was in the past, so He knows how we handled similar situations. He knows whether or not we learned from that time, or if we still have some growing to do. He knows how we will handle it in the future, whether or not we will have love and concern for what is being asked for. He knows if we are ready for the request or not. Remembering this when we get a no, or not right now should help in accepting the answers to our prayers, even when it's not the answer we wanted. It should be of great comfort to know that He is everywhere, sees all, and knows all.

> *"The Peace of God, that passes all understanding, will guard your hearts and your minds in Christ Jesus." - Philippians 4:7*

Peace is something that most people would like to have, but may rarely truly pursue correctly. It can only be found in Christ Jesus. We can learn to be content in all situations when we trust all of God's answers. Just as Paul learned in Philippians 4:11, *"Not that I speak in regard to need, for I have learned in whatever state I am, to be content."* Too often peace is sought after in other ways such as self-help books, quiet time, yoga, etc. These things are temporary or will be of no help. Maybe it is sought after briefly, but not held fast to. True peace is found only in him. It's everlasting and eternal. When his peace dwells in us, we learn that whatever his answer is, it's what is best and what is right. If only God knows the reasons why, that is just fine because He is my Father who only wants the best for me and gives the best to me. He allows situations to happen because He knows what is needed at the time. Whether we see it as good or bad is of no consequence. God knows it is for our good. That should give an overwhelming sense of relief... relief to not be anxious, to not overstep and step out of pocket, making life harder than it has to be because we are straying from his peace separating ourselves from him. Staying in line with his will allows us to keep his peace, keeping us one with him.

Sadly, many ignore his will and decide to assume or try to justify their actions with the lie that "He didn't answer." He may have just answered "No" or "not right now." Emotions can often get in the way, fog up our thoughts of getting to the truth of the matter and feelings end up overriding the facts. This is also important to remember when we have a clear "Yes." Receiving a yes answer when we get exactly what we asked for comes easy. We may be quick to say, "The Father knows best" here, but being careful to not get a haughty spirit in those times we receive the answers we desire is essential. *"For who makes you differ from another? And what do you have that you did not receive? Now if you did indeed receive it, why do you boast as if you had not received it" (1 Corinthians 4:7).* If we aren't careful, we could begin to fall into Satan's trap by assuming the yes was because we are so right. Yes, it may be a reward for being righteous but we wouldn't have it unless the Lord decided to give it. Satan's goal is to deceive us, to convince us that we have arrived at a place where we are always right, that we are so successful in ALL we do, that our thinking is superior to others or most importantly, superior to the Father's thoughts. He wants us to brag about what we have received because we are more like him that way. We may also fall into the trap that what we are thinking is true, when it may not be.

The Lord blesses us even when we are wrong. He may still allow us to have what we asked for, for various reasons. His allowing our requests could be a part of trying to get us to humble ourselves, to get us to wake up and acknowledge the fact that He is right and we are wrong. *"We all have sinned and fall short of the glory of God" (Romans 3:23).* Psalm 81:12 says, *"I gave them over to their own stubborn heart. To walk in their own counsels."* In the passages prior to this we see God telling the people how He was the one who has continued to deliver them, protect and provide for them, and fill them up with all they need. He is pleading with them to listen to his voice, to not follow other gods, and to not have other gods in their hearts. But they would not listen. They chose to go their own way. Verse 12 tells us He allowed them to have their way, to go the way they thought was right. Proverbs 14:12 warns, *"There is a way that seems right to a man, but its end is the way of death."* Death isn't just physical. We can live a spiritually dead life when we live thinking that we are always right and have somehow arrived to a point in life that we are so blessed materially because we are so right. Forgetting to humble oneself in the midst of blessings means we still have learning to do. We will never arrive to a point that we won't need any guidance from the Creator because we know the right way all on our own. That is thinking like Satan. One who humbles himself will not say, "I have this or that because I am being obedient." That will be apparent to those who know us. Humility recalls that we only know right because of God telling us what is right. Are we giving God the credit for that, thanking him for the right way? Our thankfulness for the right way will be evident in our actions that display his right way.

"You ask and you receive not because you ask amiss, that you may spend it on your pleasures" (James 4:3). Asking "amiss" may be the reason as to why God's answer is no or not right now because we were asking for the wrong reasons. We weren't asking for things that we needed but things that we wanted. This mindset is askew. He knows exactly where our thinking is when we ask. He knows if we are asking for his glorification or our own. We very well could have received it because we did ask for his glorification. On the other hand, He knows that it could lead to idolatry, to worship the things instead of the One who gave us the things. It could cause us to think we acquired these things by something that we did, dismissing altogether that we have what we have because the Lord allowed us to have it. He could have allowed us to have things we ask for that give us pleasure because there may be a lesson, or a wakeup call to a dangerous mind set. He then gives us over to our own desires in hopes we would change. He wants us to keep in mind that without him we would have nothing (1 Corinthians 4:7). He always gives us what we need, and when we ask for our wants, it needs to be balanced with spiritual thinking instead of carnal. An example of this would be wanting a new car to carry forth his will by making myself available to get others to worship or various meetings or activities to learn more about the Word. Asking for something so that He may be glorified, and remembering that God knows our intentions, would definitely be to his glorification. Being deliberate and intentional when it comes to all we are asking for will help us to ask for his glory and not our own. Remembering that all his answers are given according to what He knows about us and our lives will help us to prepare our minds and to properly weigh what we are asking for and why.

Denial, Justification, Rebellion

Without acceptance of God's will for our lives we begin to go through a state of denial and justification of sin… together this causes rebellion. Many refuse to even learn what God's will for them actually is; therefore, they do not know what they need to accept. They refuse to seek that part of his word. Refusal to seek what his word says on anything is denying that God has provided us with all we need pertaining to life and godliness and that is rebelling against God, *"as His divine power has given to us all things that pertain to life and godliness, through the knowledge of Him who called us by glory and virtue,"* (2 Peter 1:3).

Paul in his zeal was rebelling against God believing he was justified. But he found out how wrong he was on the road to Damascus. He realized just how much harm he had done because of his refusal to seek the truth of what God really had desired of him. *"And He said, who are you Lord? And the Lord said, I am Jesus whom you are persecuting. It is hard for you to kick against the goads"* (Acts 9:5). The Strong's definition for goads is prick or sting. The Lord is telling Saul as He is about to transform to Paul, he is making it hard fighting against what is right. Every time he does, it is like a sting or a prick. Jesus is giving him a chance to stop fighting against him but rather to work with him. While Paul's journey with the Lord is not absent of pain and persecution for turning his life around, he understood the persecution he received in Christ was gain for doing what was right. Oftentimes rebellion occurs because we fail to see what we are gaining and only see it as what we are losing. What it really boils down to is not being ready to give up what the world sees as gain or what we may have been used to thinking is gain.

Sin takes us further than we ever thought or imagined it could. We can end up trying to justify our sins. Not seeking his will and/or ignoring his will leads to a justification in our minds. We try to rationalize our ungodly emotions and thoughts. The example earlier of one pursuing a relationship for all the wrong reasons, such as their looks, education level, status, is an example I have heard Christians use to justify their rebellion. They say, well "he is not a Christian but he does have a Master's degree and a good job, he works out so he is healthy, and he will come around to become a Christian in due time." It's as if that last sentence is supposed to override it all. They are trying to justify this pursuit of what makes them happy over what is right and pleasing to the will of the Father. If we continue to pursue a relationship or situation that does not draw us closer to God, we are deceiving ourselves (and usually end up deceiving others including the one being sought after), into thinking that what we are doing is bringing others to Christ, therefore glorifying Christ. We may be attempting to become the example of a Christian to one or to many. However, if we are not seeking God's will constantly and consistently, then we are actively seeking the will of ourselves, influenced by Satan. There is no justification in that. *"Put on the whole armor of God, that you may be able to stand against the wiles of the devil" (Ephesians 6:11).* Instead of being transformed by the renewing of our minds through his will, we are conformed to the world. *"And be not conformed by this world but be ye transformed by the renewing of your mind." Romans 12:2*. Nothing is setting us apart from the world when we conform. We look like everyone else with that behavior. Transformation is noticeable to others because it is so different from what they are used to seeing. Renewal is needed daily. Our example of this is with the Bereans who searched the scriptures daily to see if these things were so according to Acts 17:11. They were noble-minded the scripture says. They were ready to know what the Word said and not accept their own thoughts and wishes. They wanted to know if these thoughts and desires they had, along with what they were now being taught, were in accordance with what God says. As his children, when we do not seek him, we are rebelling against him. Rebellion is a scary place to be because we are deceiving ourselves, and we are in danger of losing our souls. When we are in rebellion, we are influencing others to follow us in mocking God. God will not be mocked. *"Do not be deceived, God is not Lmocked. For whatever a man sows that he will also reap" (Galatians 6:7-8)*. There is a price to pay for rebellion. *"Therefore whoever resists the authority resists the ordinance of God and those who resist will bring judgement upon themselves" (Romans 13:2)*. Taking others with us to destruction is just what Satan wants; he is trying to take with him as many as he can. Our influence on others is vitally important to our soul salvation. Our mission is to seek and save the lost. We will cause possible ruin to other souls because we are not saving them by leading them to destruction. It's dangerous to be in a place of rebellion for any amount of time. For our life is like a vapor. *"Whereas you do not know what will happen tomorrow. For what is your life? It is even a vapor that appears for a little time and then vanishes away"* (James 4:14). We do not know the time we will leave these earthly bodies. If we are in a state of rebellion and die before we're reconciled back to an upright state in Christ, all of our chances are gone and we will be lost.

Questions to Ponder

1. Name I willing to humble myself to allow God to perfect me into spirituality or am I going to continue to fall into carnality?

2. How often am I examining myself to ensure that his word is dwelling within me?

3. When was the last time I sacrificed my will for the Father's will?

4. What harm have I done to myself or to others because of my turning a blind eye, and what am I willing to do to correct this behavior?

5. Have I been or am I currently rebelling against God and trying to justify my reason?

Chapter 7 - *My Resolve*

"But Daniel purposed in his heart that he would not defile himself with the portion of the Kings' delicacies, nor with the wine which he drank; therefore, he requested of the chief of the eunuchs that he might not defile himself." (Daniel 1:8)

    Purposed here means resolved. To be resolved is having a firm purpose or intent. Having designed a resolution. Daniel was determined and set his mind on his purpose and what God's purpose for him was. He and his friends, Shadrach, Meshach, and Abed-Nego, who also stood firm in their resolve with him here, are also found later in the third chapter of Daniel standing firm against the king. These four boys were chosen by Nebuchadnezzar, who was a pagan king, to be a part of his special court. Nebuchadnezzar desired to become the most powerful king known to the Babylonian empire. He confined the city of Jerusalem and took with him whatever and whomever he wished. Daniel and the other three Hebrew boys were part of what the king asked the master of the eunuchs, Ashpenaz, to capture for him. The king wanted *"some of the children of Israel and some of the king's descendants and some of the nobles"* (Daniel 1:3). Daniel and his friends were first captured from their home in Jerusalem and taken to Babylon. This would be an honor for some to be chosen to be a part of the king's court at that time and still today. It meant you already stood out from most in some fashion, that you had special qualities. Daniel 1:4 says, *"young men in whom there was no blemish, but good-looking, gifted in all wisdom, possessing knowledge and quick to understand, who had ability to serve in the King's palace, and whom they might teach the language and literature of the Chaldeans."* These qualities set them apart according to the standard of men and kings in their day as well as this present time because it fulfills a desire of men to be held in high regard. But what really set Daniel and his friends apart from the rest and made them special was their resolve. Daniel knew what would come with this learning of the Chaldeans customs. He would have to compromise his own beliefs and customs. He would have to conform to the Chaldeans. He chose to stand firm on his faith in God. He knew that conforming was not an option. They all were given new names that now would connect them to the new way they were learning. Daniel did not allow this new given name to stick, nor did others that knew him. They knew how dedicated he was to God. The new name they gave him was Belteshazzar which means Bel, the pagan god, protects. Daniel's birth name means God-honoring. He realized that he would be dishonoring God by claiming a false god was protecting him, when he wholeheartedly knew the God of Jerusalem was the true protector. Daniel was not going to let his heart be changed. He was protective of his heart and mind, as we should be according to Proverbs 4:23, *"Watch over your heart with all diligence. For out of it are the issues of life."* If he was to follow along with their customs and names, Daniel knew his heart would be turned from God. He was aware that it would be extremely hard to hold on to his resolve and integrity by following their customs. If we compare it to trying to live for the world and living for Christ, it is just impossible. We cannot serve men and God. Part of the new customs are referred to in Daniel 1:5 and 1:8. They consisted of eating special meats and special wines, only made so by the fact they were coming from a king who had the best of the best. In Jewish custom they were not to eat meat or drink wine. He was not going to be moved from his resolve and chose to abide by all the Jewish law, not just certain parts. So, he requested of the prince of the eunuchs that he not defile himself by following these new customs. The prince wanted to know what made Daniel think that he should receive different treatment than all the rest? Daniel asked him to let him prove that they would look the best out of all if he allowed him his request and if he did not, he was ready to be dealt with accordingly. The prince granted his request (Daniel 1:9-14). What would have been seen as just a simple change to those who are not watching over their hearts, to accept what the king has given, Daniel was not willing to do. He concerned himself with what he had been taught. His mind was set on doing what was right by God, glorifying Him in obedience, and faith exhibiting God's purpose, not his own or the king's. This resolve by Daniel and the other three Hebrew boys moved them to stand up and out for God's glory. We should have the same courage to display the resolve that Daniel did. Daniel 1:15 says, *"And at the end of the ten days their countenance appeared better and fatter in flesh than all the young men who ate the portion of the king's delicacies."*

When up against the whole world but more specifically Satan, we need to recognize whether or not we are standing out from the world and up for God's purpose or standing on our own will. Are we compromising on what seems insignificant to men, but is very significant to the will of God? Are we following the traditions of men who follow the prince of the air trying to live according to their standards? God wants us to live our lives according to His standards.

Keeping this in mind and applying it to how we dress would help us to follow the standards He has set forth for us. He wants us to dress modestly. *"In like manner also, that the women adorn themselves in modest apparel, with propriety and moderation, not with braided hair or gold or pearls or costly clothing" (1 Timothy 2:9).* Wearing tight, and or short anything, is not modest. Having hair, nails, extra eyelashes, clothes, jewelry, etc. that bring attention to us because of their brand name, look, and/or cost, is not modest or in moderation. We don't have to look like the world, and as a matter of fact, we should not. We are not standing out by looking like everyone else. I like how the KJV of this verse says, "adorn themselves with shamefacedness and sobriety." One cannot be shamefaced or sober by drawing attention to themselves adorned in immodesty. If we did, we would realize this does not represent God and his holiness, but rather it only represents and serves our carnal thinking; therefore, Christians should not partake. He wants us to appreciate the way He made our bodies, and not to be overly concerned with our looks. He expects us to value how He created us and not try to enhance or change it distorting his creation. Romans 12:1 says, *"I beseech you therefore, brethren, by the mercies of God that you present your bodies a living sacrifice, holy, acceptable to God, which is your reasonable service."*

"But Daniel purposed in his heart that he would not defile himself with the portion of the Kings' delicacies, nor with the wine which he drank; therefore, he requested of the chief of the eunuchs that he might not defile himself" (Daniel 1:8). Purposed here means resolved. To be resolved is having a firm purpose or intent; having designed a resolution. Daniel was determined and set his mind on his purpose and what God's purpose for him was. Daniel was mentally wide awake, he was sober minded, aware of what would defile him. Titus 2:11-12 says, *"For the grace of God that brings salvation has appeared to all men, teaching us that, denying ungodliness and worldly lusts, we should live soberly, righteously, and godly in the present age."* This is how Daniel chose to stand; soberly, righteously, and godly. His resolve was in the fact that God would hold him up and save him. He was doing what was right in the sight of God. He was not concerned with what his outward appearance was to others. Daniel had his mind set on doing what was right by God, by glorifying God in obedience and faith exhibiting God's purpose.

Daniel was strengthened by God's will, and he displayed great courage. He was an example to others around him and they trusted him because of his faith. This situation could have gone bad...but because Daniel had favor, mainly from God...his determination and desire to glorify God showed in the results of his godly decision. He did not haphazardly act, he acted on what he knew of the Father's will and committed himself to it. *"Commit your way to the Lord, trust also in Him, and he shall bring it to pass" (Psalm 37:5).*

Queen Esther is a beautiful example of one who was resolved to save her people, who were God's chosen people, when she went before the king. She knew the cost could be death. Esther was also chosen by a king, King Ahasuerus in Esther chapter 2. This king was looking for a new queen after his previous one disrespected him by not honoring his wishes. Ahasuerus appointed officers that would gather young beautiful virgins to Shushan. The virgins had to go through vigorous cleansing and purification processes in order to go before the king in order to be chosen for queen. Ultimately, she was loved above all the others by Ahasuerus, and she gained the crown of queen in Esther 2:17. Esther, who was brought up by her uncle Mordecai after both her parents died, was commanded not to show her heritage of being a Jew while undergoing the process of purification before becoming queen. After being chosen she still had not let it be known. Shortly after becoming queen, Mordecai, who sat inside the king's gate, became aware of a plot to kill the king by two of his doorkeepers. He informed Esther who informed the king. And consequently, the plotters were both hanged (Esther 2:19-23). In chapter 3 another plot was formed by one of the king's princes, Haman. Haman was a very trusted prince. However, when Haman saw that Mordecai would not bow or pay homage to him as everyone else did inside the king's gate, he despised Mordecai and wanted to let his wrath out on him. Haman instead learned that he was a Jew and decided to take his wrath out on all of the Jews in the whole kingdom. Haman went to the king and tricked him into creating a decree against anyone who did not follow his laws to be killed. He knew this would cover the Jews but did not tell the king the exact story. So, because the king trusted him, he put forth the decree. News reached Mordecai and he tore his clothes and put on sackcloth, Esther 4:1. Esther was then made aware of her uncle's mourning but did not know the reason for it. She sent clothing to him but he wouldn't receive it. She decided to call upon Hathach, the king's chamberlain that was chosen to attend to her. She sent him to see what was wrong with Mordecai. When Hathach returned he had the decree that was to destroy the Jews. His message to her was to go to the king and request supplication. Her message back was no one was to go to the king without being called and would be put to death unless the king held out the golden scepter to them. Esther had not been called. She could lose her life for disobeying the king's commands. Mordecai received the message and let her know in Esther 4:13-14 *"Do not think in your heart that you will escape in the King's palace, any more than all the Jews. For if you remain completely silent at this time, relief and deliverance will arise for the Jews from another place, but you and your father's house will perish. Yet who knows whether you have come to the kingdom for such a time as this."* After she fasted with her maids and Mordecai with the Jews of Shushan, she was resolved to go unto the king. Her response was, "if I perish, I perish" at the end of chapter 4:16. She knew the cost could be death. She had great strength under tremendous consequence. But saving others because it was right is what allowed her to move through any anxiety about the situation. She understood it was greater than her, and saving her people was the right thing to do.

    Christians, we must be so resolved in what we believe, that we are willing to stand even if we are the only ones standing. Maybe we are THE one called at that very moment to work on behalf of our Savior. We are His chosen vessels to deliver His message of deliverance for our fellow Christians who may need to return to the Lord. Likewise, for those that are lost in the world, we may be there so they might hear His message of deliverance to gain salvation. Even though the book of Esther does not mention God's name, it is important to remember that this book was placed in His divine word for our learning. So, it should not be lost that God was with her, it was God that strengthened her, and gave her the courage to stand. Esther was a Jew. She was willing to sacrifice her life just as Jesus who was still to come would later do. God knew His plans and He used Esther to become an example for us. We should be so resolved in our minds that it moves us to take action for God and His people. Our thoughts about what we want should fall to the wayside.

Stop laying aside God's will and returning to vomit

"As a dog returns to his own vomit, So a fool repeats his folly" (Proverbs 26:11). If we want to ensure that we do not keep making the same mistakes over and over, going through horrible situation one after another, falling down the path of sin and destruction, then we must lay aside our will, and walk in the Lord's will. Allow Him to guide us. Go back to what you know! As Christians we have been washed and cleansed of the filth of the world. To stay white as snow, we must continue to be washed in the word. *"…that He might sanctify and cleanse her with the washing of water by the word,"* (Ephesians 5:26). We are refusing to change when we keep repeating bad, ungodly behavior. A dog returning to his vomit sounds pretty disgusting. Right? Well, that is exactly how God sees it. It is hard to fathom a person doing this, but when we think about it that way, it brings a lot of clarity. Change can only occur when we acknowledge our wrongs, admit we were relying on our will, and not the Father's will. Laying aside our will allows growth to our spiritual maturity. We have to make a conscious effort to daily put aside our will. Keeping the Lord's will in the forefront of our mind will help us on this journey. It is not a one and done kind of deal. It is a daily, purposeful effort. In praying to God every day, throughout the day, letting Him know you desire to do His will and not yours, you will find the joy, peace, understanding and contentment that will help your journey go much smoother.

Whom will you serve?

If we are not choosing the Lord's will, we are choosing our own and we just cannot have it both ways. We must choose one to be pleasing to the Father. *How long will we waver between two opinions? And Elijah came to all the people, and said, "How long will you falter between two opinions? If the Lord is God, follow Him; but if Baal, follow him." But the people answered him not a word (1 Kings 18:21). "And if it seems evil to you to serve the Lord, choose for yourselves this day whom you will serve, whether the gods which your fathers served that were on the other side of the River, or the gods of the Amorites, in whose land you dwell. But as for me and my house, we will serve the Lord" (Joshua 24:15).*

Compromise is faltering between two opinions trying to balance our opinion or the opinion of man with the Word of God. There is no balance there. It cannot be done. Compromise also happens when there is still a desire to hang on to the ways of the world. This is called spiritual weakness or immaturity. We have not yet begun to live soberly in this place. If we were sober, we would not even think about trying to compromise with the world. James 1:8 addresses this problem as "double minded and unstable in all his ways". We cannot halfway serve God. As the saying goes "Ain't no half steppin'." As a child of God, we should want to serve Him so we are not lost. We are sure of the way we want to follow and have made up our mind that God is the only way to assure stability. Recall the times that we went our own way when we chose to separate ourselves from Him to serve our own purposes. Remembering this and the consequences that followed should make us firm in our decision that true life is only in Jesus.

Questions to Ponder

1. Are we so resolved in our purpose that we are not concerned with what others think of us?

2. Are we as sober as Daniel, knowing what defiles us and not partaking in it?

3. Do we repeat the same destructive behavior constantly?

4. Would we take a stand so strong that we would give up our life for others as Esther did?

5. Have we learned to not compromise the way of the Lord?

Chapter 8 - Gaining and Maintaining Sobriety

Gaining and maintaining sobriety requires constant purposeful effort. It was never promised to have an easy life, but a blessed righteous life through obedience. Once we make up our mind to live soberly, we must continue to be on the lookout for Satan. He won't go away easily; he wants to retrieve us back into his clutches. He will use everyone he can, including ourselves to get us back. We must be mindful to not let his tricks allow us to go back to straddling the fence. We can't just pay lip service, talking about how blessed we are in all ways, then when difficulty comes, abandon the blessings the Lord has set up for us to deal with these difficulties. Our blessings don't stop because difficulties come. We must continue to be thankful and appreciative of the blessings the Lord has allowed us to have. Learning to be thankful always in all situations is necessary. It will help to keep our minds focused on "the Author and Finisher of our faith" (Hebrews 12:2). When we are thankful the focus goes back to the Father which helps us to remember that He has the final say in all and through all. Everything will work out for good (according to His definition), because He is providing for us…and He still gives us more than we deserve to be thankful for. Most importantly, all that we still have has been given to us in order to carry out His will because that is our purpose.

At times we may find ourselves going through many difficulties and life just seems out of control. But we have a hope, faith and trust in the Lord's will! HE is control! Be anxious for nothing. What we can do at these times is be sober about the work we have done in our hearts and examine if we are applying what we have learned. We can make sure our lives are worthy of our calling and that what we are sharing with others is being applied to our own lives. Automatic mode should kick in during difficult times because we are aware that we will go through trials…in 1Peter 4:12 we are told, *"Beloved, do not think it strange concerning the fiery trial which is to try you, as though some strange thing happened to you."* Verse 13 says, *"but to rejoice to the extent that you partake of Christ's sufferings, that when His glory is revealed, you may also be glad with exceeding joy."* I am reminded of a song created from 2 Corinthians 5:7 and Ephesians 2:8. It says, "for we walk by faith and not by sight, we are saved by grace, not by might." For we are walking not by our physical sight but our spiritual sight. Our spiritual sight comes from our faith and trust in Him. Only because He graciously gave us the opportunity to be saved through Him. We have been given all that we need pertaining to life and godliness. Spiritual thinking leads to spiritual living, spiritual living leads to obedience.

It allows us to get out of our own way, but most importantly the Lord's way. What does that look like? Decreasing so that He can increase. That means when we are working for the Lord whether in our local congregation or in our personal jobs… we aren't being discouraging, we aren't bickering, complaining, gossiping, or being a hindrance but rather a vessel that the Lord can use, mold and contribute to. We are letting Him transform our lives so that His light can shine bright, bringing souls to Him. It means committing to putting Him first, getting ME out of the way. Going back to the when we decided to put on Christ, we were ready to be molded. Light that fire again. Sounds easy enough right? But it proves to be made difficult over and over. It's not about what I want but what His will is, and what He wants for us. I must stop talking and offering opinions on situations. Job had to realize this in Job 40:3-5. He realized this after challenging God about his situation, speaking as if he could do something that God couldn't do, or as if he had power all on his own, let alone better than God's Almighty power. He realized that he needed to put his hand over his mouth and say nothing else. He realized he was wrong. He was overstepping his position. He understood in that moment that he needed to step back and allow God to work from His perspective, not his own. God has a seat above our situations. He can see what we cannot. Therefore, we must step back and re-position ourselves as a student and a servant. Job realized he still had learning to do, and so do we.

    A student is humble, eager to learn and then willing to apply what they have learned. We are students of Christ. We are on a continual journey of learning and growing from His word, the words of life. When we have made up our minds to study for anything, such as a degree or a job, we set aside time for that. Studying God's word is MORE important than even those things. Without knowing and understanding God and what He desires for us, we can't do anything else properly or efficiently. If the Word has everything pertaining to life, then we treat it as such. We will be blessed if we hunger and thirst after righteousness, and we will be filled according to one of the beatitudes from Matthew 5:6. We show that we truly believe by applying His teaching to everything in the life He has blessed us with, including the hard times. Yes, even those are blessings because God allows them to perfect us and give us more practice and more application time. Difficult times are times that stick out to those in the world. They see how we handle them. If we are handling them as a blessed child of God, they see Jesus. His light draws them. They wonder what is it that keeps Christians going through such heartache, tragedy, and trial. Then they can ask us about that hope we have and we can share it with them. That is how His message is shared, through all we do on a daily basis. There is no time off. We are always expected to be working for Him, and we should be glad to do it. Being concerned about convenience of situations can dim His light, because we are not decreasing but rather we are increasing, blocking His light. If we are unwilling to be inconvenienced, we have made it about us. Jesus was not concerned with being inconvenienced or uncomfortable. His mind was settled on the Father's will.

"Study to show thyself approved unto God a workman that needeth not be ashamed rightly dividing the word of Truth" (2 Timothy 2:15 KJV). The Strong's definition of the word study here is to use speed, that is to make effort, be prompt, give diligence to, be diligent; give an honest effort, don't delay, make it constant, consistent. That means set aside time to do it. We set aside time to do what we want. This should include study of God's word. If we truly have a desire to mature, to know the will of God, apply it and teach it to others, we will make the time. We cannot expect to grow if we aren't studying. When life gets hectic and study time starts to decrease or things start trying to move in on your time, do your best to not let it. First pray about it. Ask the Lord to help you see the adjustments that you may need to make. Let Him know that your desire is to keep Him first and not let anything deter you from that. There is a song that says "He will make a way, because He is the way maker!" So true are these words.

In all things and situations PRAY! Pray without ceasing (1 Thessalonians 5:17)! Without ceasing. Wow. That is a lot. That tells us just how important prayer is to be in our lives. If we want to have a spiritual life, prayer must be in it. It's our way of communicating with Him, our way of petitioning on others behalf, for ourselves and for constant thankfulness to Him. When going into prayer we must have full faith and assurance that He hears, and that He answers our prayers. Any request we have we should take to Him (Ephesians 6:18). As Christians, we live each day by faith. We are to be trusting and hopeful in each and every blessing that comes our way through Him. We rest our cares and burdens in His hands and we leave them there. Our faith works in knowing that He understands, He sees, He cares, He hears, and He KNOWS. Therefore, we don't have anything to worry about. Whatever His answer is, we know it is best (Proverbs 16:1). The more we lean on our faith, by communicating with Him, reading and studying His word, and submitting to the Holy Spirit, we will produce the fruit of the Holy Spirit and we will be sober and obedient to Christ. By submitting to the Holy Spirit, we will experience the transformation the Lord wants to see! We can do nothing on our own (2 Peter 1:21).

Transformation is also facilitated through the family the Lord has provided through His church. If we want to stay sober and remain sober, we have to connect to the support group we are given. We are commanded to worship each and every Sunday (Hebrews 10:25). That is where we come together to grow together, to encourage one another in what we heard taught and from any studies that were conducted outside of worship time. This is the new family for our new way of living. Whether we are new Christians, we fell away, or are continuing in the faith, we take one day at a time walking hand in hand with the Lord and the family He has given us. We are all on the same journey striving to live soberly to please the Father. Again, going back to the point that "Father Knows Best" and He gives us all we need, fellowship is another example of that. He knew that we would need like-minded family in Him to bear one another's burdens, to encourage, and for support. He tells us to *not be unequally yoked with unbelievers. For what fellowship has righteousness with unrighteousness* (2 Corinthians 6:14). Together with fellow Christians we are striving to live in His marvelous light. To be made righteous through Him we have decided to *"stand therefore, having girded your waist with truth, having put on the breastplate of righteousness"* (Ephesians 6:14). Those who have not humbled themselves and submitted to His way of being a Christian are unrighteous. Once we are put in right standing by Christ, it is our responsibility to stay in right standing. It has been said that "Heaven is ours to lose" after the moment of baptism. We have to continue in the faith. *"Now he who keeps his commandments abides in Him and He in Him. And by this we know that He abides in us, by the Spirit whom He has given us"* (1John 3:24). Being unequally yoked does not keep you in right standing. So, we should avoid it, because it makes us opposed to God (James 4:4). The unrighteous do not live in the light. *"What communion has light with darkness"* (2 Corinthians 6:14)? None. The two do not co-exist. Think of a light being turned on in a dark room. Anything exposed to the light is in the light. There is no more darkness until the light is turned out. We turn out the light by trying to join with unrighteousness. We are to be in the world but not of the world. Our lives are to teach the world that they might be saved and come into His light and be made right. That's it. Fellowship is from God, through Him, with Him, with His people, and for Him and His people. He wanted us to have fellowship with those who have the same goal in mind, which is obedience to God. Thayer Lexicon defines fellowship as association, community, communion, joint participation, the share which one has in anything. The unrighteous have no goal to be obedient to God. *"The Spirit of truth, whom the world cannot receive, because it neither sees Him, nor knows Him; but you know Him, for He dwells with you and will be in you"* (John 14:17). Fellowship is the sharing of the hope we have in Christ, building one another up in order to grow, helping one another to not fall and when we do, being there with open arms welcoming one another into the fold. Only the righteous will know who to point to. Every opportunity we have that we are able to fellowship, we ought to take advantage of. Fellowship works best when we are open to the love of Christ through His saints, and we are open to learn from one another and not be offended easily. If we are closed off, not wanting to communicate and share His word and our lives, it will be working against what we have been given to be closer to God. How do we help one another if we aren't getting to know each other? We won't know there is a problem or a need if we do not know one another. No, we won't be very close to every member, but we should make every effort to reach out to one another when the time presents itself. We are not in fellowship with God and certainly not our brother if we hate our brother or sister. *"If someone says, "I love God, and hates his brother, he is a liar; for he who does not love his brother whom he has seen, how can he love God whom he has not seen" (1 John 4:20).* In the same vein, if we sit on the same pew as someone and purposely do not speak, there is a heart issue. You cannot say you are being Christ-like and in fellowship with Him when you purposely avoid someone. Fellowship brings us all together; it does not separate.

In order to Sober Up, we must be keenly aware of our mistakes and be willing to fix them. Together with our hands in the Master's hands we can live soberly and righteously in obedience!

Questions to Ponder

1. Have I allowed Satan to influence me into falling for his tricks?

2. Am I working with the body to spread the gospel or am I being contentious?

3. How often do I pray and do I worry about what I have prayed about or am I assured the Lord hears me?

4. Am I spending time with the family that the Lord has blessed me with, in every opportunity possible or am I joining myself with the unrighteous?

5. What have I put into practice to achieve and maintain sobriety?

Notes

About the Authors

Regina Braden resides in Columbus, Ohio and attends the Watkins Rd. church of Christ. She has had the pleasure of serving the Lord's church as a youth counselor, presenter, teacher, program coordinator, choral director, and member of acapella groups. Regina has presented at Ladies' Day programs, Youth Conferences, the Ohio State Lectureship, and National Lectureship of the churches of Christ.

Currently, Regina is actively involved at the Watkins Rd congregation where she teaches teenage girls and the ladies bible study. She also directs the choral group – The Voices of Watkins Rd.

Regina is employed by Huntington National Bank as a Vice President/Customer Research Program Manager Senior. She received both her BBA and MBA degrees from the University of Cincinnati, and is a certified Temperament Counselor and Life Coach.

A single Christian woman, Regina enjoys reading, quilting, and traveling.

One of Regina's favorite scriptures is John 16:33 - "These things I have spoken to you, so that in Me you may have peace. In the world you have tribulation, but take courage; I have overcome the world."

Heather Hougland was born and raised in Oberlin, Ohio. She comes from a long line of Christians with her family starting the first congregation (in the Lorain County area of Ohio) in her Great Aunt's home in Oberlin. This congregation later formed into the Clinton Ave congregation in Elyria, Ohio. She became a Christian at the age of 13 and shortly after began assisting and teaching Sunday School classes. She was also part of the a cappella groups in the congregation, and as an adult, became a youth counselor at her home congregation.

Throughout her 30 years of being a Christian, she has continued to stay involved in and contributing to the work of the Lord through: evangelizing, contributing to the creation of a ministry for single moms, assisting with clothing and food giveaways, participating in several acapella groups, assisting and teaching new convert classes, speaking for a ladies day and a youth rally, directing personal one on one bible studies, group bible studies at a local homeless shelter for women, children and families, co-developing the exercise group at the homeless shelter as well as serving in other capacities of outreach within the shelter, leading vacation bible school programs, assisting with the lunch program provided at the congregation, assisting in developing in home youth monthly bible studies, working with the youth in various capacities, and visiting the sick/shut-in and elderly.

Heather is a licensed massage therapist and studied health and wellness at Kaplan University. Heather has opened two massage businesses through the years, including one in North Carolina and another in Columbus. She is now working as a massage therapist for Capital City Hospice and Kinsale Golf and Fitness club. She is the mother of two boys, and also has three grandchildren. She and her youngest son have been active members of the Watkins Rd congregation for over seven years. At Watkins Rd, her faith has grown and her resolve has deepened. Heather is always looking and praying for opportunities to spread the gospel and encourage her brothers and sisters in Christ on their spiritual walk. She has found being involved in the work also encourages her in the faith.

A favorite scripture of hers is Philippians 3:12 - "Not that I have attained, or am already perfected; but I press on, that I may lay hold of that for which Christ Jesus has also laid a hold of me.

Aisha Jenya was born in Columbus, OH and raised in the church of Christ from a youth.

She is a long-time member of the Watkins Rd. church where she has served as a bible class teacher for teen girls. She welcomes opportunities to participate in the congregation's teaching program and has also led several studies for the Ladies' Bible class as well as studies for women and children at a local homeless shelter. Aisha has participated as a speaker for a Ladies Day Program and youth workshop hosted by her home congregation. She has also volunteered at Fort Hill Christian Youth Camp as a youth counselor and teacher. She seeks to be involved in various areas of service and ministry while striving to be a faithful Christian, active and available to work of the church.

Aisha received her Bachelor of Accounting from the DeVry Institute of Technology (University) and MBA from Ohio Dominican College (University) and is currently employed as a Tax Examiner Specialist for the State of Ohio. She enjoys time and fellowship with family and friends, and the joy of being a mother to her college-aged daughter.

Aisha is also the author of "Are You Thirsty?", a workbook exploring common thirsts or desires youth, and adults alike, are challenged with in life.

One of Aisha's favorite scriptures is Romans 8:28 – "And we know that all things work together for good to those who love God, to those who are called according to His purpose."

www.ingramcontent.com/pod-product-compliance
Lightning Source LLC
Chambersburg PA
CBHW060852050426
42453CB00008B/952